UNDERSTANDING SOFTWARE

Max Kanat-Alexander on simplicity, coding, and how to suck less as a programmer

Max Kanat-Alexander

BIRMINGHAM - MUMBAI

UNDERSTANDING SOFTWARE

First published: September 2017

Production reference: 1270917

Published by Packt Publishing Ltd.
Livery Place
35 Livery Street
Birmingham B3 2PB, UK.

ISBN 978-1-78862-881-5

www.packtpub.com

CREDITS

Author
Max Kanat-Alexander

Acquisition Editor
Dominic Shakeshaft

Content Development Editor
Dominic Shakeshaft

Editor
Amit Ramadas

Indexer
Pratik Shirodkar

Production Coordinator
Arvindkumar Gupta

Cover Work
Arvindkumar Gupta

ABOUT THE AUTHOR

Legendary code guru Max Kanat-Alexander brings you his writings and thoughts so that your code and your life as a developer can be healthy, and embrace simplicity. Why make life hard when making software can be simple?

WWW.PACKTPUB.COM

eBooks, discount offers, and more

Did you know that Packt offers eBook versions of every book published, with PDF and ePub files available? You can upgrade to the eBook version at www.PacktPub.com and as a print book customer, you are entitled to a discount on the eBook copy. Get in touch with us at customercare@packtpub.com for more details.

At www.PacktPub.com, you can also read a collection of free technical articles, sign up for a range of free newsletters and receive exclusive discounts and offers on Packt books and eBooks.

https://www.packtpub.com/mapt

Get the most in-demand software skills with Mapt. Mapt gives you full access to all Packt books and video courses, as well as industry-leading tools to help you plan your personal development and advance your career.

Why subscribe?

- ♦ Fully searchable across every book published by Packt
- ♦ Copy and paste, print, and bookmark content
- ♦ On demand and accessible via a web browser

CUSTOMER FEEDBACK

Thanks for purchasing this Packt book. At Packt, quality is at the heart of our editorial process. To help us improve, please leave us an honest review on this book's Amazon page at `https://www.amazon.com/dp/1788628810`.

If you'd like to join our team of regular reviewers, you can e-mail us at `customerreviews@packtpub.com`. We award our regular reviewers with free eBooks and videos in exchange for their valuable feedback. Help us be relentless in improving our products!

TABLE OF CONTENTS

Foreword vii

Part One: Principles for Programmers

Chapter 1: Before You Begin... 3

    If You're Going To Do It Then Do it Well 5

Chapter 2: The Engineer Attitude 7

Chapter 3: The Singular Secret of the
Rockstar Programmer 11

Chapter 4: Software Design, in Two Sentences. 15

Part Two: Software Complexity and its Causes

Chapter 5: Clues to Complexity 19

Chapter 6: Ways To Create Complexity: Break Your API . . . 21

Chapter 7: When Is Backwards-Compatibility
Not Worth It? 25

Chapter 8: Complexity is a Prison. 29

Part Three: Simplicity and Software Design

Chapter 9: Design from the Start 35

    Starting the Right Way. 36

Chapter 10: The Accuracy of Future Predictions 37

Chapter 11: Simplicity and Strictness 41

Chapter 12: Two is Too Many 47

    Refactoring. 49

Chapter 13: Sane Software Design. 51

    The Wrong Way 52

    The Right Way 57

    We followed all the Laws Of Software Design 60

Part Four: Debugging

Chapter 14: What is a Bug? 63

    Hardware. 64

Chapter 15: The Source of Bugs 65

    Compounding Complexity 66

Chapter 16: Make It Never Come Back. 69

    Make it Never Come Back – An Example 71

    Down the Rabbit Hole. 75

Chapter 17: The Fundamental Philosophy of Debugging . . . 77

    Clarify the Bug. 79

    Look at the System. 80

    Find the Real Cause 82

    Four Steps 83

Part Five: Engineering in Teams

Chapter 18: Effective Engineering Productivity 87

    The Solution 90

Chapter 19: Measuring Developer Productivity 99

Chapter 20: How to Handle Code Complexity in a Software Company **107**

Step 1 – Problem Lists 109

Step 2 – Meeting 110

Step 3 – Bug Reports 111

Step 4 – Prioritization 111

Step 5 – Assignment 113

Step 6 – Planning 113

Chapter 21: Refactoring is about Features **115**

Being Effective 116

Refactoring Doesn't Waste Time, It Saves It 120

Refactoring To Clarity 120

Summary 122

Chapter 22: Kindness and Code **123**

Software is about People 124

Chapter 23: Open Source Community, Simplified **129**

Retaining Contributors 130

Removing the Barriers 137

Getting People Interested 140

Summary 142

Part Six: Understanding Software

Chapter 24: What is a Computer? **145**

Chapter 25: The Components of Software: Structure, Action, and Results. **149**

Chapter 26: Software Revisited: (I)SAR Clarified. 153

Structure 154

Action. 155

Results 156

ISAR in a Single Line of Code 156

Wrapping SAR Up 157

Chapter 27: Software as Knowledge. 159

Chapter 28: The Purpose of Technology 163

Are there Counter-Examples to this Rule? 164

Is the Advance of Technology "Good"? 165

Chapter 29: Privacy, Simplified 167

Privacy of Space 168

Privacy of Information 170

A Summary of Privacy. 174

Chapter 30: Simplicity and Security. 175

**Chapter 31: Test-Driven Development and the
Cycle of Observation** 179

Examples of ODA. 180

Development Processes and Productivity 181

Chapter 32: The Philosophy of Testing. 185

Test Value 186

Test Assertions. 187

Test Boundaries 187

Test Assumptions 188

Test Design. 188

End to End Testing 189

Integration Testing 190

Unit Testing 192

Reality 193

Fakes 194

Determinism 196

Speed 197

Coverage 198

Conclusion – The Overall Goal of Testing 198

Part Seven: Suck Less

Chapter 33: The Secret of Success: Suck Less 203

Why is it that this worked?. 205

Chapter 34: How We Figured Out What Sucked 209

Chapter 35: The Power of No 213

Recognizing Bad Ideas 215

Having No Better Idea 216

Clarification: Acceptance and Politeness 217

Chapter 36: Why Programmers Suck 219

What to Study 223

Chapter 37: The Secret of Fast Programming:
Stop Thinking 227

Understanding 228

Drawing 229

Starting 230

Skipping a Step. 231

Physical Problems 231

Distractions 232

Self-Doubt 232

False Ideas 233

Caveat 233

Chapter 38: Developer Hubris. 235

Chapter 39: "Consistency" Does Not Mean "Uniformity" . .239

**Chapter 40: Users Have Problems,
Developers Have Solutions** 241

Trust and Information. 242

Problems Come from Users. 243

Chapter 41: Instant Gratification = Instant Failure. 245

Solving for the long term 246

How to Ruin Your Software Company 247

**Chapter 42: Success Comes from Execution,
Not Innovation.** 249

Chapter 43: Excellent Software 251

1. Does exactly what the user told it to do. 252

2. Behaves exactly like the user expects it to behave 253

3. Does not block the user from communicating
   their intention 255

Excellence is senior to (but is not in conflict with)
code simplicity. 257

Index 259

FOREWORD

I started writing on www.codesimplicity.com in 2008 for one reason only – I wanted to make the world of software development a better place. I wasn't trying to be famous, or get contracting jobs, or push some ideology on people. My intention was purely to help people.

What I had observed was that there was a lot of opinion in the field of software engineering, but not a lot of facts or basic principles. Now, this might seem like a shocking statement to some people, because surely software development is a scientific field where we all know exactly what we're doing – we work with highly technical machines and we use a lot of complex systems to accomplish our jobs. There *must* be a science to it, right?

Well, the problem is that in order to be a science you must have *laws* and a system of organized information based on those laws. Usually, you also must demonstrate that your laws and your system actually *work* without exception in the physical universe. It's not sufficient to just have some information about technology. You must have *basic principles*.

There are many ways to derive these basic principles. The most popular and accepted way is through the scientific method. There are other ways, too. The whole subject of how you discover these things is covered by a study called "epistemology," which is a word that means "the study of how knowledge is known." For example, you know your name. *How* do you know that that is your name? How do you know that's true? If you wanted to understand how to build a house, what would you do to gain that knowledge? And so on.

I'm sort of over-simplifying it, and perhaps some philosophy professors will come after me and write bad reviews because I'm not *really* explaining epistemology or how I used it, but I hope that what I've written here is enough for the common reader to get that what I wanted was some *method* that would lead to the development of *basic principles*. Various methods of epistemology, including the scientific method, helped me discover these.

My first book, *Code Simplicity*, is a description of those basic principles of software development. But there's more to know than just those basics. True, you *could* derive everything there is to know about software design from those laws in *Code Simplicity*, but since I've already derived a lot of stuff from them, why not just share that with you now?

This book is a collection of my writings since *Code Simplicity*, as well as some additional content that I wrote before *Code Simplicity* but which didn't really fit in that book. Most of the content in this book is also on my website, but in this book it's been organized, curated, and edited for maximum readability. Also, you get to read it in book format, which is often easier to digest and understand.

There is one chapter in the book that is not on my website and never will be — the one called "Excellent Software." I actually wrote it years ago as part of the first draft of Code Simplicity, but could never bring myself to give it away for free.

The book doesn't have to be read in order. It's designed so that it reads nicely if you go from page to page and read each section in sequence, but you can also skip around and read any of the sections you want if you think some part will be more interesting than another.

To help both kinds of readers, I've split the book into a few parts. That way, people reading in order get a consistent flow, and people who want to skip around know what each part covers.

The first three parts of the book cover some foundational principles of being a programmer and then get into aspects of software complexity and simplicity. After that comes "Engineering in Teams," a whole new set of principles developed since *Code Simplicity* based on my experience successfully applying the principles of *Code Simplicity* across large engineering organizations.

Then comes a section where I write about the philosophy behind the principles of software design, "Understanding Software." This includes the article "The Philosophy of Testing," which is a more thorough coverage of the basic principles of testing than was found in my first book.

Then comes the section "Suck Less," based on one of my most popular blog articles of all time. It starts off explaining why "Suck Less" works as a philosophy for product management in software development, and then goes on to talk about how you can make your software suck less and specific ways to become a better programmer yourself.

Overall, the whole point of the book is to help you be a better software developer, and that is the *only* point. I would much rather live in a world where software is simple, well-designed, reliable, fast, and easy to make, wouldn't you? In this book and *Code Simplicity*, I've told you how to do it – all you have to do is apply the data that I've given you.

Best of luck.

Max Kanat-Alexander

August 2017

— PART ONE —

PRINCIPLES FOR PROGRAMMERS

1

BEFORE YOU BEGIN...

One of the major goals that I have with researching software design is the hope that we can take people who are "bad programmers" or mediocre programmers and, with some simple education and only a little experience, bring them into being good programmers or great programmers.

I want to know — what are the fundamental things you have to teach somebody to make them into a great programmer? What if somebody's been programming for years and hasn't gotten any better — how can you help them? What are they missing? So I've written quite a bit about that in this book, particularly in *Part Seven - Suck Less*.

However, before somebody can even *start* on the path of becoming a better software developer, one thing has to be true:

> **In order to become an excellent programmer, you must first *want* to become an excellent programmer. No amount of training will turn somebody who does not *want* to be excellent into an excellent programmer.**

If you are a person who is passionate about software development — or even just somebody who likes being good at their job — it may be hard to understand the viewpoint of somebody who simply doesn't want to get any better. To fully grasp it, it can be helpful to imagine yourself trying to learn about some area that you personally have no desire to be great in.

For example, although I admire athletes, enjoy playing soccer, and sometimes enjoy watching sports in general, I've never had a desire to be a great athlete. There's no amount of *reading* or *education* that will ever turn me into a great athlete, because I simply don't want to be one. I wouldn't even read the books in the first place. If you forced me to take some classes or go to some seminar, it would leave my mind as soon as I took it in, because I would simply have no desire to know the data.

Even if I was playing sports every day for a living, I'd think, "Ah well, I don't have any passion for athletics, so this information simply isn't important to me. Some day I will be doing some other job, or some day I will retire and not have to care, and until then I'm just going to do this because they pay me and it's better than starving."

As hard as this can be to imagine, that is what happens in the minds of many "bad" programmers when you tell them how or why they should write better code. If they don't sincerely want to be the best programmers that they can be, it *does not matter* how much education you give them, how many times you correct them, or how many seminars they go to, they *will not get better.*

If You're Going To Do It Then Do it Well

So what do you do? To be fair, I may not be the best person to ask — if I'm going to do something, I feel that I should do my best to excel in it. Perhaps the best thing you can do is encourage people to follow that concept.

You could say to them something like: "If you're going to be doing it anyway, why not do it well? Wouldn't it at least be more enjoyable to be doing this if you were more skilled at it? What if some other people were impressed with your work, how would that feel? Would it be nice to go home at the end of the day and feel that you had done something well? Would your life be better than it is now, even if only a little? Would your life get *worse*?"

However you do it, the bottom line is that people must be interested in improving themselves before they can get better. How you bring them up to that level of interest doesn't really matter, as long as they get there *before* you waste a lot of time giving them an education that they're just going to throw away as soon as they hear it.

-Max

2

THE ENGINEER ATTITUDE

The attitude that every engineer should have, in every field of engineering, is:

> **I can solve this problem the right way.**

Whatever the problem is, there's always a *right way* to solve it. The right way can be known, and it *can be* implemented. The only valid reason ever to not implement something the right way is *lack of resources*. However, you should always consider that the right way does exist, you are *able* to solve the problem the right way, and that given enough resources, you *would* solve the problem the right way.

The "right way" usually means "the way that accounts for all reasonably possible future occurrences, even unknown and unimaginable occurrences."

A bridge that could stand up to any reasonably possible environmental condition or any reasonably possible amount of traffic without constant maintenance would be built the "right way."

> **Software code that maintained its simplicity while providing the flexibility needed for reasonably possible future enhancements would be designed the "right way."**

There are lots of invalid reasons for not solving a problem the right way:

♦ **I don't know the right way.** Often this just requires more understanding or study, to figure out the right way. When I run into this situation, I walk away from the problem for a while, and then often I'll come up with the solution when I'm just out walking, or the next day when I come back to it. I try not to compromise on something that isn't the right way just because I don't know what the right way is yet.

♦ **The group cannot agree on what the right way would be.** Sometimes a group of people have argued about what would be the "right way" and the subject has gotten very confused. Groups are not very good at making decisions. As we all know, you don't design software by committee, and I suspect that "design by committee" in other fields of engineering is just as bad.

The solution here is to assign an experienced and trusted engineer who understands the basic laws of the subject you're working in to determine the right way by himself or herself, probably after carefully studying the existing arguments and collecting relevant information, following standard, valid engineering procedures.

◆ **I am too lazy/tired/hungry/discombobulated to do this the right way, right now.** This happens to everybody from time to time. It's 1 in the morning, you've been working on the project for 15 hours straight, and you just need the damn thing to *work*, right now! Give it a rest, though, and come back later. The world isn't ending, and the problem will still be here and solvable later.

Go to sleep, go eat something, take a walk — do whatever it takes to get into a mental space where you're willing to solve the problem the right way, and then come back. If you're in a state where you can't solve the problem the right way, then it's really time to take a break.

You're not being delinquent in your duties if you do so — you're actually correctly taking responsibility for the success of the project by saying "this needs to be done right, and the way to do it right, right now, is to take a break and come back later".

Mostly, it all just takes the constant and continual belief in yourself that you can solve the problem the right way.

-Max

3

THE SINGULAR SECRET OF THE ROCKSTAR PROGRAMMER

Before all the laws of software, before the purpose of software, before the science of software design itself, there is a singular fact that determines the success or failure of a software developer:

> **The better you understand what you are doing, the better you will do it.**

"Rockstar" programmers understand what they are doing far, far better than average or mediocre programmers. And that is it.

This fact makes the difference between the senior engineer who can seem to pick up new languages in a day and the junior developer who struggles for ten years just to get a paycheck, programming other people's designs and never improving enough to get a promotion. It differentiates the poor programmers from the good ones, the good programmers from the great ones, and the great ones from the "rockstar" programmers who have founded whole multi-billion dollar empires on their skill.

As you can see, it isn't anything complicated, and it isn't something that's hard to know. Nor is it something that you can only do if you're born with a special talent or a "magical ability to program well." There is nothing about the *nature of the individual* that determines whether or not they will become an excellent programmer or a poor one:

> **All you have to do in order to become an excellent programmer is fully understand what you are doing.**

Some may say that they already understand everything. The *test* is whether or not they can *apply* it. Do they produce beautifully architected systems that are a joy to maintain? Do they plow through programming problems at a rate almost unimaginable to the average programmer? Do they explain everything clearly and in simple concepts when they are asked for help? Then they are an excellent programmer, and they understand things well.

However, far more commonly than believing that they "know it all", many programmers (including myself) often feel as though they are locked in an epic battle with an overwhelming sea of information. There is so much to know that one could literally spend the rest of his life studying and still come out with only 90% of all the data there is to know about computers.

> **The secret weapon in the epic battle, the Excalibur of computing knowledge, is understanding.**

The better that you understand the *most fundamental* level of your field, the easier it will be to learn the next level. The better you understand *that* level, the easier the next one after that will be, and so on. Then once you've gone from the most fundamental simplicities to the highest complexities, you can start all over again and find amazingly that there is so much more to know at the very, very bottom.

It seems almost too simple to be true, but it is in fact the case. The path to becoming an excellent programmer is simply full and complete understanding, starting with a profound grasp of the basics and working up to a solid control of the most advanced data available.

I won't lie to you — it sometimes is a long path. But it is worthwhile. And at the end of it, you may find yourself suddenly the amazing senior engineer who everyone comes to for advice. You may be the incredible programmer who solves everything and is admired by all his peers. You might even come out a "rockstar" with millions of dollars and a fantastically successful product. Who knows?

I can't tell you what to do or what to become. I can only point out some information that I've found to be truthful and valuable. What you do with it is up to you.

-Max

4

SOFTWARE DESIGN, IN TWO SENTENCES

It is possible to reduce the primary principles of software design into just two statements:

1. **It is more important to reduce the Effort of Maintenance than it is to reduce the Effort of Implementation.**

2. **The Effort of Maintenance is proportional to the complexity of the system.**

And that is pretty much *it*.

If all you knew about software design were those two principles, you could evolve every other general principle of software development.

-Max

— PART TWO —

SOFTWARE COMPLEXITY AND ITS CAUSES

5

CLUES TO COMPLEXITY

Here are clues that tell you that your code may be too complex:

1. You have to add "hacks" to make things keep working.

2. Other developers keep asking you how some part of the code works.

3. Other developers keep misusing your code, and causing bugs.

4. Reading a line of code takes longer than an instant for an experienced developer.

5. You feel scared to modify this part of the code.

6. Management seriously considers hiring more than one developer to work on a single class or file.

7. It's hard to figure out how to add a feature.

8. Developers often argue about how things should be implemented in this part of the code.

9. People make utterly nonsensical changes to this part of the code very often, which you catch only during code review, or only after the change has been checked in.

-Max

6

WAYS TO CREATE COMPLEXITY: BREAK YOUR API

An API is a sort of a promise…"You can always interact with our program this way, safely and exactly like we said." When you release a new version of your product that doesn't support the API from your old version, you're breaking that promise.

> **Above and beyond any vague philosophical or moral considerations about this, the *technical* problem here is that this creates complexity.**

Where once users of your API only had to call a simple function, now they have to do a version check against your application and call one of two different functions depending on the result. They might have to pass their parameters a totally different way now, *doubling* the complexity of their code if they keep both the old way and the new way around. If you changed a lot of functions, they might even have to re-work their whole application just to fit with the way your new API works!

If you break your API several times, their code will just get more and more and more complicated. Their only other choice is to break *their* compatibility with old versions of your product. That can make life *extremely* difficult for users and system administrators trying to keep everything in sync. You can imagine how quickly this could spiral out of control if every piece of software on your system suddenly broke its API for interacting with every other piece of software.

For *you*, maintaining an old API can be painful, and getting rid of it can make life so much simpler. But it's not complexity for you that we're talking about particularly here, it's complexity for *other programmers*.

The *best* way to avoid this problem altogether is *don't release bad APIs*. Or, even better (from the user's perspective), create some system where you promise to always maintain the old APIs, but give access to more modern APIs in a different way. For example, you can always access old versions of the salesforce.com API merely by using a different URL to interact with the API. Every time you interact with the Salesforce API, you are in fact specifying exactly what version of the API you expect to be using. This approach is a lot easier in centralized applications (like salesforce.com) than in shipping applications, because shipping applications have to care about code size and other things. Maintaining old APIs is also very difficult if you only have a small team of developers, because that maintenance really takes a lot of time and attention.

In any case, releasing an unstable or poor API is going to either complicate *your* life (because you'll then have to maintain backwards compatibility forever) or the life of your API users (because they'll have to modify all of their applications to work with both the "good" and "bad" API versions).

If you choose to break your API and not provide backwards-compatibility, remember that some API users will never update their products to use your new API. Maybe they just don't have the time or resources to update their code. Maybe they are using a tool that interacts with your product, but the maintainer of the tool no longer provides updates. In any case, if the cost of fixing *their* code is greater than the value of upgrading to new versions of your product, they could choose to remain with an old version of your product *forever*.

That can have a lot of unforeseen consequences, too. First they keep around an old version of your product. Then they have to keep around old versions of certain system libraries so that your product keeps working. Then they can't upgrade their OS because the old version of your product doesn't work on the new OS. Then what do they do if some unpatched security flaw is exploited on their old OS, but they're still tied to your old product and so can't upgrade their OS? Or some security flaw in your old product is exploited? All of these situations are things that you have to take responsibility for when you choose to break your API.

And yet, having *no* API can lead to the same situation. People create crazy "hacks" to interact with your system, and then they can't upgrade because their hacks don't work on the new version. This is not as bad as breaking your API, because you never *promised* anything about the hacks. Nobody has the right to *expect* their hacks to keep working.

But still, if management *orders* them to integrate with your product, those clever programmers will find any possible way to make it work, even if it sticks them with one version of your product forever.

So definitely make an API if you have the development resources to do it. But put a lot of careful thought into your API design before implementing it. Try actually using it yourself. Survey your users carefully and find out exactly how they want to use your API. Generally, do everything in your power to make the API as stable as possible before it's ever released. It's not a matter of spending years and years on it, it's just a matter of taking some sensible steps to find out *how* the API should really work before it's ever released.

And once it's released, please, *please*, if you can help it, don't break the API.

-Max

7

WHEN IS BACKWARDS-COMPATIBILITY NOT WORTH IT?

This title might seem a bit like a contradiction to the previous chapter...and of course, you really shouldn't break your API, if you can help it. But sometimes, maintaining backwards compatibility for *any* area of your application can lead to a point of diminishing returns. This applies to everything about a program, not just its API.

A great example of the backwards-compatibility problem is Perl. If you read the summaries of the perl5-porters mailing list, or if you're familiar with the history of the Perl internals in general, you'll have some idea of what I mean.

Perl is full of support for strange syntaxes that really, nobody should be using anymore. For example, in Perl, you're supposed to call methods on an object like `$object->method()`. But there's also a syntax called the "indirect object syntax" where you can do `method $object`. *Not* `method($object)` though — only the case without the parenthesis is the indirect object syntax.

Really, nobody should be using that syntax, and it's not that hard to fix applications to call their methods the right way. And yet that syntax is maintained and supported in the Perl binary to keep *backwards compatibility*.

Perl is full of things like this that block *forward progress* because of *historical problems*.

Now obviously, this is a balancing act. When there are a huge number of people using something, and it would be really difficult for them to change, you pretty much have to maintain backwards compatibility. But if maintaining that backwards-compatibility is really *stopping* forward progress, you need to warn people that the "old cruft" is going away and *ditch it*.

> ## The alternative is infinite backwards-compatibility and *no* forward progress, which means total death for your product.

This also gives one good reason why you shouldn't just add features willy-nilly to your program. One day you might have to support *backwards-compatibility* for that feature that you added "because it was easy to add even though it's not very useful." This is an important thing to think about when adding new features — are you going to have to support that feature forever, now that it's in your system? The answer is: *you probably are*.

If you've never maintained a large system that's used by lots of people, you might not have a good idea of:

1. How many people can be screwed over if you break backwards-compatibility, and

2. How much you can screw yourself over by having to maintain backwards-compatibility.

The ideal solution there is: just don't add features if you don't want to support them for many, many future versions to come. Sometimes it takes a lot of programming experience to make that sort of decision effectively, but you can also just look at the feature and think, "Is it *really* so useful that I want to spend at least 10 hours on it in the next three or four years?" That's a good estimate of how much effort you're going to put into backwards-compatibility, QA, and everything else for even the smallest feature.

Once you've got a feature, then maintaining backwards-compatibility is generally the thing to do. Bugzilla, a product I worked on, could, in 2014, still upgrade from version 2.8 – which was released in *1999*. But it can do that because we wrote the upgrader in such a way that old upgrader code doesn't require any maintenance – that is, we get that backwards-compatibility for *free*. We only have to add new code as time goes on for new versions of Bugzilla, we almost never have to change old code. *Free* backwards-compatibility like that should always be maintained.

> **The only time you should seriously consider ditching backwards-compatibility is when keeping it is preventing you from adding obviously useful and important new features.**

But when that's the case, you've really got to ditch it.

-Max

~ 8 ~

COMPLEXITY IS A PRISON

Sometimes, I think, people are worried that if they make their code too simple, then either:

a. **Somehow they're not demonstrating how intelligent they are, or how valuable they are, to their managers, or**

b. **The project will become so simple to work on that anybody can just steal their job!**

It's almost as though if they actually did their job right, then they'd lose it. Now, stated that way, that's obviously a nonsensical viewpoint. But, if you've ever worried about it, here's something to think about:

> **What if your code is so complex that you'll never be able to *leave* your job?**

What if you made something so complicated that nobody else could understand it? Well, then *you personally* would be tied to *that project* forever and ever. If you wanted to work on some other project at your organization, your managers would protest, "But who else will maintain this code?" Whoever was assigned after you to work on your code would constantly be walking into your new office, saying, "Hey, how does this part work?"

Maybe you have no conscience, and you'll just leave the code to some hopeless replacement and ditch the company. However, I'm guessing that *most* people would feel tied to a project if they were sure that nobody else could ever take it over successfully. And really, even if you just take off and leave, somebody's going to be calling you up and saying, "Um, hey, you know that one piece of code where..." You'll get emails from "the new guy": "Hey, I hear you wrote this code, and I have this *problem*..." If you can't make somebody else understand your code and have them truly take it over, then you're going to be stuck with a piece of that job *forever*.

In the Bugzilla Project, I did the best I could to work myself out of a job. I loved working on Bugzilla, but I don't want to be tied to it every moment of my life. I wanted to go on vacation sometimes. I wanted to write music!

You can still hear my music and songs here by the way: http://youtube.com/user/imagineeighty and http://soundcloud.com/mkanat.

I wanted to be able to leave my computer for a month, and not have the whole world collapse. So I worked to make Bugzilla simple enough and well-designed enough that somebody else could *take over* the parts I worked on, some day. Maybe then I would go on and work on other things in Bugzilla, I thought to myself, or some other programming project that I had, or maybe I would go make an album! Who knew!

> **I knew I didn't want to be imprisoned by my own code.**

If job security is so important to you that you'd tie yourself to a single job forever just to get it, then maybe you should re-evaluate your priorities in life! Otherwise, when you're making decisions about your project, one thing to remember is this:

> **Complexity is a prison; simplicity is freedom.**

-Max

— PART THREE —

SIMPLICITY AND SOFTWARE DESIGN

9

DESIGN FROM THE START

You really need to design *from the start*. You need to be working on simplicity from the very beginning of your project.

> **My policy on projects that I control is that we *never* add a feature unless the design can support it simply.**

This drives some people crazy, notably people who have no concept of the future. They start to foam at the mouth and say things like, "We can't wait! This feature is *so important!*" or "Just put it in now and we'll just clean it up later!" They don't realize that this is their *normal attitude*. They're going to say the same thing about the next feature.

> **If you don't think about the future, then *all* of your code will be poorly designed and much too complex.**

It'll be Frankenstein's monster, jammed together out of broken parts. And just like the friendly green giant, it'll be big, ugly, unstable, and harmful to your health.

Now just adding a tiny little piece and refactoring it afterward is fine. Landing a huge feature that the architecture can't support and then trying to clean it up afterward is a terrible task. Size matters.

Starting the Right Way

The worst situation is when you let people keep adding features with no design for months or years, and then one day you wake up and realize that something is not right. Now you have to fix your *whole codebase*. This is a terrible task, because just like adding a new feature, it can't be done all at once, unless you want to re-write.

If you want to start doing things the right way, you have to start doing things the *right way*. And that means that you have to fix the design piece by piece, in simple steps. That usually requires months or years of effort – totally wasted effort, because you should have just designed *from the start*. You should have thought about the future.

> **If your project lacks a strict design, and it continues to grow, then you will eventually end up over your head in complexity.**

This doesn't mean you should be designing some huge generic beast from the start that tries to anticipate all future requirements and implement them now. It means that you need to apply the principles of software design as discussed in this book and *Code Simplicity* so that you get a system that is understandable, simple, and *maintainable* from the start.

-Max

~ 10 ~

THE ACCURACY
OF FUTURE
PREDICTIONS

One thing we know about software design is that the future is important. However, we also know that the future is very hard to predict.

I think that I have come up with a theory to explain exactly how hard it is to predict the future of software.

The most basic version of this theory is:

> **The accuracy of future predictions decreases relative to the complexity of the system and the distance into the future you are trying to predict.**

As your system becomes more and more complex, you can predict smaller and smaller pieces of the future with any accuracy. As it becomes simpler, you can predict further and further into the future with accuracy.

For example, it's fairly easy to predict the behavior of a "Hello, World" program quite far into the future. It will, most likely, continue to print "Hello, World" when you run it. Remember that this is a sliding scale — sort of a *probability* of how much you can say about what the future holds. You could be 99% sure that it will still work the same way two days from now, but there is still that 1% chance that it won't.

However, after a certain point, even the behavior of "Hello World" becomes unpredictable. For example, "Hello World" in Python 2.0 in the year 2000:

```
print "Hello, World!"
```

But if you tried to run that in Python 3, it would be a syntax error. In Python 3 it's:

```
print("Hello, World!")
```

You couldn't have predicted that in the year 2000, and there isn't even anything you could have done about it if you *did* predict it. With things like this, your only hope is keeping your system simple enough that you can update it easily to use the new syntax. *Not* "flexible," *not* "generic," but simply *easy to understand and modify*.

In reality, there's a more expanded logical sequence to the rule above:

1. The difficulty of predicting the future increases relative to the total amount of change that occurs in the system and its environment across the future one is attempting to predict. (Note that the effect of the environment is inversely proportional to its logical distance from the system. For example, if your system is about cars, then changes about engines are likely to affect it, while changes in apple trees are not likely to affect it.)

2. The amount of change a system will undergo is relative to the total complexity of that system.

3. Thus: the rate at which prediction becomes difficult increases relative to the complexity of the system one is attempting to predict the behavior of.

Now, despite this rule, I want to caution you against basing design decisions around what you think will happen in the future. Remember that all of these happenings are *probabilities* and that any amount of prediction includes the ability to be wrong.

When we look only at the present, the data that we have, and the software system that we have now, we are much more likely to make a correct decision than if we try to predict where our software is going in the future. Most mistakes in software design result from assuming that you will need to do something (or never do something) in the future.

The time that this rule is useful is when you have some piece of software that you can't easily change as the future goes on. You can never *completely* avoid change, but if you simplify your software down to the level of being stupid, dumb simple then you're less likely to have to change it. It will probably still degrade in quality and usefulness over time (because you aren't changing it to cope with the demands of the changing environment) but it will degrade *more slowly* than if it were very complex.

It's true that ideally, we'd be able to update our software whenever we like. This is one of the great promises of the web, that we can update our web apps and websites instantaneously without having to ask anybody to "upgrade." But this isn't always true, for all platforms. Sometimes, we need to create some piece of code (like an API) that will *have* to stick around for a decade or more with very little change. In this case, we can see that if we want it to still be useful far into the future, our only hope is to simplify. Otherwise, we're *building in* a future unpleasant experience for our users, and dooming our systems to obsolescence, failure, and chaos.

The funny part about all this is that writing simple software usually takes *less* work than writing complex software does. It sometimes requires a bit more thought, but usually less time and effort overall. So let's take a win for ourselves, a win for our users, and a win for the future, and keep it as simple as we reasonably can.

-Max

～ 11 ～

SIMPLICITY AND STRICTNESS

As a general rule:

> **The stricter your application is, the simpler it is to write.**

For example, imagine a program that accepts *only* the numbers 1 and 2 as input and rejects everything else. Even a tiny variation in the input, like adding a space before or after "1" would cause the program to throw an error. That would be very "strict" and extremely simple to write. All you'd have to do is check, "Did they enter exactly 1 or exactly 2? If not, throw an error."

In most situations, though, such a program would be so strict as to be impractical. If the user doesn't know the exact format you expect your input in, or if they accidentally hit the spacebar or some other key when entering a number, the program will frustrate the user by not "doing what they mean."

That's a case where there is a trade-off between simplicity (strictness) and usability. Not all cases of strictness have that trade-off, but many do. If I allow the user to type in 1, One, or "1" as input, that allows for a lot more user mistakes and makes life easier for them, but also adds code and complexity to my program. Less-strict programs often take more code than strict ones, which is really directly where the complexity comes from.

> **By the way, if you're writing frameworks or languages for programmers, one of the best things you can do is make this type of user interface "non-strictness" as simple as possible, to eliminate the trade-off between usability and complexity, and let them have the best of both worlds.**

Of course, on the other side of things, if I allowed the user to type in O1n1e1 and still have that be accepted as "1", that would just add needless complexity to my code. We have to be more strict than that.

Strictness is mostly about what input you allow, like the examples above. I suppose in some applications, you could have output strictness as well: output that always conforms to a particular, exact standard. But usually, it's about what input you accept and what input causes an error.

Probably the best-known strictness disaster is HTML. It wasn't designed to be very strict in the beginning, and as it grew over the years, processing it became a nightmare for the designers of web browsers. Of course, it was eventually standardized, but by that time most of the HTML out there was pretty horrific, and still is. And because it wasn't strict from the beginning, now nobody can break backwards compatibility and make it strict.

Some people argue that HTML is commonly used because it's not strict. That the non-strictness of its design makes it popular. That if web browsers had always just *thrown an error* instead of accepting invalid HTML, somehow people would not have used HTML.

That is a patently ridiculous argument. Imagine a restaurant where the waiter could never say, "Oh, we don't have that." So I ask for a "fresh chicken salad", and I get a *live chicken*, because that's "the closest they have." I would get pretty frustrated with that restaurant. Similarly, if I tell the web browser to do something, and instead of throwing an error it tries to guess what I meant, I get frustrated with the web browser. It can be pretty hard to figure out why my page "doesn't look right," now.

So why didn't the browser just tell me I'd done something wrong, and make life easy for me? Well, because HTML is so un-strict that it's impossible for the web browser to know that I *have* done something wrong! It just goes ahead and drops a live chicken on my table without any lettuce.

Granted, I know that at this point that you can't make HTML strict without "breaking the web." My point is that we got into that situation because HTML wasn't strict *from the beginning*. I'm not saying that it should suddenly become strict now, when it would be almost impossible. (Though there's nothing wrong with slowly taking incremental steps in that direction.)

In general, I am strongly of the opinion that computers should never "guess" or "try to do their best" with input. That leads to a nightmare of complexity that can easily spiral out of control. The only good guessing is in things like Google's spelling suggestions — where it gives you the *option* of doing something, but doesn't just go ahead and *do* something for you based on that guess. This is an important part of what I mean by strictness — input is either right or wrong, it's never a "maybe." If one input could possibly have two meanings, then you should either present the user with a choice or throw an error.

> **The world of computers is full of things that should have been strict from the beginning, and became ridiculously complex because they weren't.**

Now, some applications are forced to be non-strict. For example, anything that takes voice commands has to be pretty un-strict about how people talk, or it just won't work at all. But those sorts of applications are the exception. Keyboards are very accurate input devices, mice slightly less so but still pretty good. You can require input from those to be in a certain format, as long as you aren't making life too difficult for the user.

Of course, it's still important to strive for usability – after all, computers are here to help humans do things. But you don't necessarily have to accept every input under the sun just to be usable. All that does is get you into a maze of complexity, and good luck finding your way out – they never strictly standardized on any way to write maps for the maze.

-Max

~ 12 ~

TWO IS TOO MANY

There is a key rule that I personally operate by when I'm doing incremental development and design, which I call "two is too many."

This rule is how I implement the "be only as generic as you need to be" rule from *Code Simplicity*.

> **Essentially, I know how generic my code needs to be, by noticing that I'm tempted to cut and paste some code, and then instead of cutting and pasting it, designing a generic solution that meets just those two specific needs.**

I do this as soon as I'm tempted to have two implementations of something. For example, let's say I was designing an audio decoder, and at first I only supported WAV files. Then I wanted to add an MP3 parser to the code. There would definitely be common parts to the WAV and MP3 parsing code, and instead of copying and pasting *any* of it, I would *immediately* make a superclass or utility library that did *only* what I needed for those two implementations.

The **key** aspect of this is that I did it right away — I didn't allow there to be two competing implementations; I immediately made one generic solution. Another **important** aspect of this is that I didn't make it *too* generic — the solution *only* supports WAV and MP3 and doesn't expect other formats in any way.

There's a further part of the "two is too many" rule that goes exactly like this:

> **A developer should ideally never have to modify one part of the code in a similar or identical way to how they just modified a different part of it.**

That is, a developer should not have to "remember" to update Class A when they update Class B. They should not have to know that if Constant X changes, you have to update File Y. In other words, it's not just two *implementations* that are bad, but also two *locations*. It isn't always possible to implement systems this way, but it's something to strive for.

If you find yourself in a situation where you *have* to have two locations for something, make sure that the system fails loudly and visibly when they are not "in sync." Compilation should fail, a test that always gets run should fail, etc. It should be impossible to let them get out of sync.

And of course, the simplest part of the "two is too many" rule is the classic principle: "Don't Repeat Yourself." So don't have two constants that represent the same exact thing, don't have two functions that do the same exact thing, etc.

There are likely other ways that this rule applies. The general idea is that when you want to have two implementations of a single concept, you should somehow make that into a single implementation instead.

Refactoring

When refactoring, this rule helps find things that could be improved and gives some guidance on how to go about it. When you see duplicate logic in the system, you should attempt to combine those two locations into one. Then if there is *another* location, combine that one into the new generic system, and proceed in that manner.

That is, if there are *many* different implementations that need to be combined into one, you can do incremental refactoring by combining two implementations at a time, as long as combining them does actually make the system simpler (easier to understand and maintain). Sometimes you have to figure out the best order in which to combine them to make this most efficient, but if you can't figure that out, don't worry about it — just combine two at a time and usually you'll wind up with a single good solution to all the problems.

It's also important *not* to combine things when they shouldn't be combined. There are times when combining two implementations into one would cause more complexity for the system as a whole or violate the **Single Responsibility Principle**, which states that any given module, class, or function should represent only *one* concept in the system.

For example, if your system's representation of a Car and a Person have some slightly similar code, don't solve this "problem" by combining them into a single CarPerson class. That's not likely to decrease complexity, because a CarPerson is *actually* two different things and *should* be represented by two separate classes.

"Two is Too Many" isn't a hard and fast law of the universe – it's more of a strong guideline that I use for making judgments about design as I develop incrementally. However, it's quite useful in refactoring a legacy system, developing a new system, and just generally improving code simplicity.

-Max

⌒ 13 ⌒

SANE SOFTWARE DESIGN

I have come up with an analogy that should make the basic principles of software design understandable to everybody. The great thing about this analogy is that it covers basically everything there is to know about software design.

Imagine that you are building a structure out of lead bars. The final structure will look like this:

```
       |
  _|_|_|_
       |
       |
       |
```

You have to build the structure and put it up at a certain location, so that people can use it for something.

The lead bars represent the individual pieces of your software. Putting it up at the location is like putting your software into production (or sending it out to your users). Everything else should be fairly clear as to how it translates to software, if you think about it. You don't have to translate everything to software in your mind as you read, though. Everything should be quite clear if you just imagine that you really are just building a structure out of lead bars.

The Wrong Way

Imagine that you were building this all by yourself, and that you had to make the bars yourself out of raw metal. Here's the wrong way to build it:

1. Make one tall lead bar, and lay it flat on the ground in your workshop:

2. Cut a hole through the tall bar, and measure that hole.

3. Make a new bar that will fit through that hole:

    _____

4. Put that new bar through the hole and weld them together permanently:

5. Cut two holes in the horizontal bar, measure them, and make two new lead bars that will fit in those individual holes:

6. Insert the two bars into the horizontal bar, and weld them together permanently:

7. With a forklift, put this into a truck to move it to the location where it's supposed to be. (It's too heavy to move by yourself.)

8. With a pulley, make the construction stand upright and put it into the ground.

9. Discover that it won't stay up by itself, but if you put some blocks next to it as an emergency solution, it doesn't fall over:

10. Three days later, watch the structure fall over and break because the blocks aren't actually a permanent solution.

11. Unfortunately, part of the horizontal bar has snapped, and you have to fix it. This is difficult because the bars are all welded together, so you can't easily take out the bar and replace it with another one. You either have to build a whole new structure or weld together the broken bar. Welding the broken halves together creates a weak bond, but it's cheaper than building a whole new structure, so you just weld them.

12. Put stronger blocks next to the structure to keep it up.

13. Next week, the weather breaks the welded bars. Weld them back together again.

14. In six days, watch the structure fall over because blocks are not a permanent solution.

15. Repeat the last few steps until you run out of money or time.

Analysis of The Wrong Way

So, what was *good* about the above process? Well, it did allow one person to successfully complete a structure. In software terms, that one person "made something that works." It also created a lot of work for one person, which is good if that one person wanted a lot of work.

What was bad about it?

♦ The bars all had to be custom made in sequence, individually.

♦ Problems with the final structure (that it wouldn't stay up) were only discovered after it was entirely built and in place.

♦ When problems were discovered, they were just "quick fixed" without planning for the future.

♦ It took enormous effort to move the completed structure into place.

♦ If we ever had to change the configuration of the bars, we couldn't, because they're welded together. We'd have to build a whole new structure.

♦ The completed structure requires frequent attention.

And I'm sure we could come up with other faults. This whole analogy (including the parts below) could be analyzed all day.

Bringing It To a Group

The biggest problem with the Wrong Way process is that it wouldn't work *at all* if there were multiple people working on the project (as there usually are in real-world software projects). The main problem is that you had to measure all the holes before you built a bar, so everything had to be done by one person, in order.

There are, generally, two ways to solve this problem:

1. Write a specification for the sizes of all the individual holes beforehand, and then spread out the work of making all the different bars for each hole.

   This is problematic because one person has to write this specification, and if this were a large project (imagine thousands of holes instead of just three or four), it would take a lot of time. Nobody else on the team can be working until the specification is completed. The spec could be full of mistakes – there are as many chances for mistakes as there are holes specified, so if there are thousands of holes, that's a lot of chances for errors to be made.

2. Just say, "All bar holes will always be the same size and in the same places on the bars. Bars can be screwed together." Then set everybody to making bars with standardized holes (or go buy them from the store).

   That is simple, and it gets everybody working at once. Because you've standardized your bars, you've lost a little flexibility in dealing with any special cases that come up (maybe a half-width hole would be more useful in some part of the structure).

However, you should be able to build a decent structure entirely with standard holes, so that's not too much of a problem. And when you have a standard, you can make specific exceptions in some places more easily than if things are not standardized.

Of course, with this method it is very important that you do a little research to pick a good hole size and good bars.

This doesn't solve all of the problems of the wrong way, but it starts to put us on the track of solving the problem the right way.

The Right Way

So, what would our process look like for many people all using standardized bars that screw together? (This is the right way to build something.)

1. Have your team all go build (or buy) standardized individual bars. You can have as many people working simultaneously as there are bars in the structure.

2. Have them test their individual bars to make sure that they won't break.

3. Have them carry their individual bars to the place where the structure needs to be.

4. Put the first bar into the ground, standing upright:

|

5. Push on the first bar from all angles to see if it is going to fall over.

6. Screw in a second bar to the first one:

7. Test the complete structure now, only to find that it's not strong enough to stand by itself.

8. Attach unbreakable steel ropes to the sides of the structure, like so:

   These ropes should be able to withstand anything within reason, or even well beyond reason.

9. Test it again and find out that it now can stay up no matter how hard you push on it.

10. Add a third bar, and put new ropes on so that it looks like this:

11. Remove the lower ropes:

(Anybody who's been involved in a large refactoring project can remember doing a lot of things that sound *just like* these last two steps.)

12. Test it again.

13. Continue these steps until you have a completed structure:

14. When a pipe breaks in three months, figure out what was wrong with that pipe, fix the problem, and replace it with a new pipe that fits into the same holes. The structure is just as strong as it was before.

15. Continue the above process until you no longer have to pay attention to the structure and it just stays up all by itself.

16. Adjust the structure as necessary for the changing requirements of the users of the structure, which is easy because the holes are all standardized.

We followed all the Laws Of Software Design

♦ We thought about the future. We did that for the entire process, but we particularly did it when we put on unbreakable steel ropes that would last no matter what happened in the future.

Also note that we didn't try to *predict* the future, we just followed our principles so that no matter what happened, our structure was going to stay together and be easy to build.

♦ We allowed for change by screwing the bars together instead of welding them. We also put standardized holes in all the bars, even if we didn't need them, in case we needed to add more bars in the future.

♦ In every step of creating the structure, we kept our changes small and tested everything as we went. Creating each individual bar was a small task, and we put them together in small steps.

♦ And of course, the most important decision we made was to keep it simple by making all the holes consistent and standard, and keeping each piece small and simple.

Whether you are one person or a thousand, whether your project is 10 lines of code or 10 million, translate this process and those principles into software development, and it will work.

-Max

—Part Four—

Debugging

~14~

WHAT IS A BUG?

Okay, most programmers know the story — way back when, somebody found an actual insect inside a computer that was causing a problem. (Actually, apparently engineers have been calling problems "bugs" since earlier than that, but that story is fun.)

> **But really, when we say "bug" what *exactly* do we mean?**

Here's the precise definition of what constitutes a bug:

1. The program did not behave according to the **programmer's intentions,** or

2. The programmer's intentions did not fulfill common and reasonable user expectations.

So usually, as long as the program is doing what the programmer intended it to do, it's working correctly. Sometimes what the programmer intended it to do is totally surprising to a user and causes him some problem, so that's a bug.

Anything else is a *new* feature. That is, if the program does exactly what was intended in exactly the expected fashion, but it doesn't do *enough*, that means it needs a new "feature." That's the difference between the definition of "feature" and "bug."

Note that hardware can have bugs too. The programmer's intention is rarely "the computer now explodes." So if the programmer writes a program and the computer explodes, that's probably a bug in the hardware. There can be other, less dramatic bugs in the hardware, too.

Essentially, anything that causes the programmer's intentions to not be fully carried out can be considered a bug, unless the programmer is trying to make the computer do something it wasn't designed to do.

For example, if the programmer tells the computer "take over the world" and it wasn't designed to be able to take over the world, then the computer would need a new "take over the world" feature. That wouldn't be a bug.

Hardware

With hardware, you also have to think about the *hardware designer's* intentions, and common and reasonable *programmer* expectations. At that level, software programmers are actually the main "users", and hardware designers are the people whose intentions we care about.

Of course, we also care about the normal user's expectations, especially for hardware that users interact with directly like printers, monitors, keyboards, etc.

-Max

～ 15 ～

THE SOURCE OF BUGS

Where do bugs come from? Could we narrow down the cause of all bugs to just one source or a few? As it turns out, we can.

> **Bugs most commonly come from somebody's failure to reduce complexity. Less commonly, they come from a misunderstanding of something that was actually simple.**

Other than typos, I'm pretty sure that those two things are the source of all bugs, though I haven't yet done extensive research to prove it.

When something is complex, it's far too easy to misuse it. If there's a black box with millions of unlabeled buttons on it, and 16 of them blow up the world, somebody's going to blow up the world. Similarly, in programming, if you can't easily understand the documentation of a language, or the actual language itself, you're going to misuse it somehow.

There's no *right* way to use a box with millions of unlabeled buttons, really. You could never figure it out, and even if you wanted to read the 1000-page manual, you probably couldn't remember the whole thing well enough to use the box correctly. Similarly, if you make anything complex enough, people are more likely to use it wrongly than to use it correctly. If you have 50, 100, or 1000 of these complex parts all put together, they'll never work right, no matter how brilliant an engineer puts them together.

> **So do you start to see here where bugs come from? Every time you added some complexity, somebody (and "somebody" could even be you, yourself) was more likely to misuse your complex code.**

Every time it wasn't *crystal clear* **exactly** what should be done and how your code should be used, somebody could have made a mistake. Then you put your code together with some other code, and there was another chance for mistakes or misuse. Then we put more pieces together, etc.

Compounding Complexity

Often, this sort of situation happens: the hardware designer made the hardware really complicated. So it had to have a complicated assembly language. This made the programming language and the compiler really complicated. By the time you got on the scene, you had no hope of writing bug-free code without ingenious testing and design. And if your design was *less than perfect*, well...suddenly you have lots of bugs.

This is also a matter of understanding the viewpoint of other programmers. After all, something might be simple to *you*, but it might be complex to somebody who isn't you.

If you want to understand the viewpoint of somebody who doesn't know anything about your code, find the documentation of a library that you've never used, and read it.

Also, find some code you've never read, and read it. Try to understand not just the individual lines, but what the whole program is doing and how you would modify it if you had to. That's the same experience people are having reading your code. You might notice that the complexity doesn't have to get very high before it becomes frustrating to read other people's code.

Now, once in a while, something is really simple, and the programmer just misunderstood it. That's another thing to watch for. If you catch a programmer explaining something to you in a way that makes no sense, perhaps that programmer misunderstood something somewhere along the line. Of course, if the thing he was studying was extremely complex, he had basically no hope of fully understanding it without a PhD in *that thing*.

So these two things are very closely related. When you write code, it's partially your responsibility that the programmer who reads your code in the future understands it, and understands it easily. Now, he could have some critical misunderstanding — maybe he never understood what "if" meant. That's not your responsibility.

Your responsibility is writing clear code, with the expectation that the future programmer reading your code understands the basics of programming and the language you're using.

So, there are a couple of interesting rules that we can conclude here:

1. **The simpler your code is, the fewer bugs you will have.**

2. **Always work to simplify everything about your program.**

-Max

~16~

MAKE IT NEVER COME BACK

When solving a problem in a codebase, you're not done when the symptoms stop. You're done when the problem has disappeared and will **never come back**.

It's very easy to stop solving a problem when it no longer has any visible symptoms. You've fixed the bug, nobody is complaining, and there seem to be other pressing issues. So why continue to do work on it? It's fine for now, right? No.

> **Remember that what we care about the most in software is the future.**

The way that software companies get into unmanageable situations with their codebases is not really handling problems until they are done.

This also explains why some organizations cannot get their tangled codebase back into a good state. They see one problem in the code, they tackle it until nobody's complaining anymore, and then they move on to tackling the next symptom they see. They don't put a framework in place to make sure the problem is never coming back. They don't trace the problem to its source and then make it *vanish*. Thus their codebase never *really* becomes "healthy."

This pattern of failing to fully handle problems is very common. As a result, many developers believe it is impossible for large software projects to stay well-designed — they say, "All software will eventually have to be thrown away and re-written."

This is not true. I have spent most of my career either designing sustainable codebases from scratch or refactoring bad codebases into good ones. No matter how bad a codebase is, you can resolve its problems. However, you have to understand software design, you need enough manpower, and you have to handle problems until they will never come back.

In general, a good guideline for how resolved a problem has to be is:

> **A problem is resolved to the degree that no human being will ever have to pay attention to it again.**

Accomplishing this in an *absolute* sense is impossible – you can't predict the entire future, and so on – but that's more of a philosophical objection than a practical one. In most practical circumstances you can effectively resolve a problem to the degree that nobody has to pay attention to it now and there's no immediately-apparent reason they'd have to pay attention to it in the future either.

Make it Never Come Back – An Example

Let's say you have a web page and you write a "hit counter" for the site that tracks how many people have visited it. You discover a bug in the hit counter – it's counting 1.5 times as many visits as it should be counting. You have a few options for how you could solve this:

1. **You could ignore the problem.**

   The rationale here would be that your site isn't *very* popular and so it doesn't matter if your hit counter is lying. Also, it's making your site look more successful than it is, which might help you.

   The reason this is a bad solution is that there are many future scenarios in which this could again become a problem – particularly if your site becomes very successful. For example, a major news publication publishes your hit numbers – but they are false. This causes a scandal, your users lose trust in you (after all, you knew about the problem and didn't solve it) and your site becomes unpopular again. One could easily imagine other ways this problem could come back to haunt you.

2. **You could hack a quick solution.**

   When you display the hits, just divide them by 1.5 and the number is accurate. However, you didn't investigate the underlying cause, which turns out to be that it counts 3x as many hits from 8:00 to 11:00 in the morning. Later your traffic pattern changes and your counter is completely wrong again. You might not even notice for a while because the hack will make it harder to debug.

3. **Investigate and resolve the underlying cause.**

   You discover it's counting 3x hits from 8:00 to 11:00. You discover this happens because your web server deletes many old files from the disk during that time, and that interferes with the hit counter for some reason.

   At this point you have another opportunity to hack a solution — you could simply disable the deletion process or make it run less frequently. But that's not *really* tracing down the underlying cause. What you want to know is, "Why does it miscount just because something else is happening on the machine?"

   Investigating further, you discover that if you interrupt the program and then restart it, it will count the last visit again. The deletion process was using so many resources on the machine that it was interrupting the counter two times for every visit between 8:00 and 11:00. So it counted every visit three times during that period. But actually, the bug could have added infinite (or at least unpredictable) counts depending on the load on the machine.

You redesign the counter so that it counts reliably even when interrupted, and the problem disappears.

Obviously the right choice from that list is to investigate the underlying cause and resolve it. That causes the problem to vanish, and most developers would believe they are done there. However, there's still more to do if you really want to be sure the problem will never again require human attention.

First off, somebody could come along and change the code of the hit counter, reverting it back to a broken state in the future. Obviously the right solution for that is to add an automated test that assures the correct functioning of the hit counter even when it is interrupted. Then you make sure that test runs continuously and alerts developers when it fails. Now you're done, right?

Nope. Even at this point, there are some future risks that have to be handled.

The next issue is that the test you've written has to be easy to maintain. If the test is hard to maintain – it changes a lot when developers change the code, the test code itself is cryptic, it would be easy for it to return a false positive if the code changes, etc. – then there's a good chance the test will break or somebody will disable it in the future.

Then the problem could again require human attention. So you have to assure that you've written a maintainable test, (see *Chapter 32, The Philosophy of Testing*), and refactor the test if it's not maintainable. This may lead you down another path of investigation into the test framework or the system under test, to figure out a refactoring that would make the test code simpler.

After this you have concerns like the continuous integration system (the test runner) – is it reliable? Could it fail in a way that would make your test require human attention? This could be another path of investigation.

All of these paths of investigation may turn up other problems that then have to be traced down to *their* sources, which may turn up more problems to trace down, and so on. You may find that you can discover (and possibly resolve) all the major issues of your codebase just by starting with a few symptoms and being very determined about tracing down underlying causes.

Does anybody really do this? *Yes*. It might seem difficult at first, but as you resolve more and more of these underlying issues, things really do start to get easier and you can move faster and faster with fewer and fewer problems.

Down the Rabbit Hole

Beyond all of this, if you really want to get adventurous, there's one more question you can ask: why did the developer write buggy code in the first place? Why was it possible for a bug to ever exist? Is it a problem with the developer's education? Was it something about their process? Should they be writing tests as they go? Was there some design problem in the system that made it hard to modify? Is the programming language too complex? Are the libraries they're using not well-written? Is the operating system not behaving well? Was the documentation unclear?

Once you get your answer, you can ask what the underlying cause of *that* problem is, and continue asking that question until you're satisfied. But beware: this can take you down a rabbit hole and into a place that changes your whole view of software development. In fact, theoretically this system is unlimited, and would eventually result in resolving the underlying problems of the entire software industry. How far you want to go is up to you.

-Max

~ 17 ~

THE FUNDAMENTAL PHILOSOPHY OF DEBUGGING

Sometimes people have a very hard time debugging. Mostly, these are people who believe that in order to debug a system, you have to think about it instead of *looking* at it.

Let me give you an example of what I mean. Let's say you have a web server that is silently failing to serve pages to users 5% of the time. What is your reaction to this question: "Why?"

Do you immediately try to come up with some answer? Do you start guessing? If so, you are doing the wrong thing. The right answer to that question is: **"I don't know."** And this gives us the first step to successful debugging:

> **When you start debugging, realize that you do not already know the answer.**

It can be tempting to think that you already know the answer. Sometimes you can guess and you're right. It doesn't happen very often, but it happens often enough to trick people into thinking that *guessing the answer* is a good method of debugging.

However, most of the time, you will spend hours, days, or weeks guessing the answer and trying different fixes with no result other than complicating the code. In fact, some codebases are full of "solutions" to "bugs" that are actually just guesses — and these "solutions" are a significant source of complexity in the codebase.

Actually, as a side note, I'll tell you an interesting principle. Usually, if you've done a good job of fixing a bug, you've actually caused some part of the system to go away, become simpler, have better design, etc. as part of your fix. I'll probably go into that more at some point, but for now, there it is. Very often, the best fix for a bug is a fix that actually deletes code or simplifies the system.

But getting back to the process of debugging itself, what *should* you do? Guessing is a waste of time, imagining reasons for the problem is a waste of time — basically most of the activity that happens *in your mind* when first presented with the problem is a waste of time. The only things you have to do with your mind are:

1. Remember what a working system behaves like.

2. Figure out what you need to look at in order to get more data.

Because you see, this brings us to the most important principle of debugging:

> **Debugging is accomplished by gathering data until you understand the cause of the problem.**

The way that you gather data is, almost always, by *looking* at something. In the case of the web server that's not serving pages, perhaps you would look at its logs. Or you could try to reproduce the problem so that you can look at what happens with the server when the problem is happening. This is why people often want a "reproduction case" (a series of steps that allow you to reproduce the exact problem) — so that they can *look* at what is happening when the bug occurs.

Clarify the Bug

Sometimes the first piece of data you need to gather is what the bug *actually is*. Often users file bug reports that have insufficient data. For example, let's say a user files the bug, "When I load the page, the web server doesn't return anything."

That's not sufficient information. What page did they try to load? What do they mean by "doesn't return anything?" Is it just a white page? You might *assume* that's what the user meant, but very often your assumptions will be incorrect. The less experienced your user is as a programmer or computer technician, the less well they will be able to express specifically what happened without you questioning them. In these cases, unless it's an emergency, the first thing that I do is just send the user back specific requests to clarify their bug report, and leave it at that until they respond. I don't look into it *at all* until they clarify things.

If I did go off and try to solve the problem before I understood it fully, I could be wasting my time looking into random corners of the system that have nothing to do with any problem at all. It's better to go spend my time on something productive while I wait for the user to respond, and then when I *do* have a complete bug report, to go research the cause of the now-understood bug.

As a note on this, though, don't be rude or unfriendly to users just because they have filed an incomplete bug report. The fact that you know more about the system and they know less about the system doesn't make you a superior being who should look down upon all users with disdain from your high castle on the shimmering peak of Smarter-Than-You Mountain. Instead, ask your questions in a kind or straightforward manner and just get the information. Bug filers are rarely intentionally being stupid – rather, they simply don't know and it's part of your job to help them provide the right information. If people frequently don't provide the right information, you can even include a little questionnaire or form on the bug-filing page that makes them fill in the right information. The point is to be helpful to them so that they can be helpful to you, and so that you can easily resolve the issues that come in.

Look at the System

Once you've clarified the bug, you have to go and look at various parts of the system. *Which* parts of the system to look at is based on your knowledge of the system. Usually it's logs, monitoring, error messages, core dumps, or some other output of the system. If you don't *have* these things, you might have to launch or release a new version of the system that provides the information before you can fully debug the system.

Although that might seem like a lot of work just to fix a bug, in reality it often ends up being faster to release a new version that provides sufficient information than to spend your time hunting around the system and guessing what's going on without information. This is also another good argument for having fast, frequent releases – that way you can get out a new version that provides new debugging information quickly. Sometimes you can get a new build of your system out to just the user who is experiencing the problem, too, as a shortcut to get the information that you need.

Now, remember above that I mentioned that you have to remember what a working system looks like? This is because there is another principle of debugging:

> **Debugging is accomplished by comparing the data that you have to what you know the data from a working system should look like.**

When you see a message in a log, is that a normal message or is it actually an error? Maybe the log says, "Warning: all the user data is missing." That looks like an error, but really your web server prints that every single time it starts. You have to know that a *working* web server does that. You're looking for behavior or output that a *working* system does not display.

Also, you have to understand what these messages *mean*. Maybe the web server optionally has some user database that you aren't using, which is why you get that warning – because you *intend* for all the "user data" to be missing.

Find the Real Cause

Eventually you will find something that a working system does not do. You shouldn't immediately assume you've found the cause of the problem when you see this, though. For example, maybe it logs a message saying, "Error: insects are eating all the cookies." One way that you could "fix" that behavior would be to delete the log message. Now the behavior is like normal, right? No, wrong – the actual bug is still happening.

That's a pretty stupid example, but people do less-stupid versions of this that don't fix the bug. They don't get down to the basic cause of the problem, as I explain in *Chapter 16, Make It Never Come Back*. Instead they paper over the bug with some workaround that lives in the codebase forever and causes complexity for everybody who works on that area of the code from then on.

It's not even sufficient to say "You will know that you have found the real cause because fixing that fixes the bug." That's pretty *close* to the truth, but a closer statement is:

> **"You will know that you have found a real cause when you are confident that fixing it will make the problem never come back."**

This isn't an absolute statement – there is a sort of scale of how "fixed" a bug is. A bug can be more fixed or less fixed, usually based on how "deep" you want to go with your solution, and how much time you want to spend on it. Usually you'll know when you've found a decent cause of the problem and can now declare the bug fixed – it's pretty obvious. But I wanted to warn you against papering over a bug by eliminating the symptoms but not handling the cause.

And of course, once you have the cause, you fix it. That's actually the simplest step, if you've done everything else right.

Four Steps

So basically this gives us four primary steps to debugging:

1. Familiarity with what a working system does.

2. Accepting that you don't already know the cause of the problem.

3. Looking at data until you know what causes the problem.

4. Fixing the cause and not the symptoms.

This sounds pretty simple, but I see people violate this formula all the time. In my experience, *most* programmers, when faced with a bug, want to sit around and think about it or talk about what might be causing it – both forms of guessing.

It's okay to talk to other people who might have information about the system or advice on where to look for data that would help you debug. But sitting around and *collectively* guessing what could cause the bug isn't really any better than sitting around and doing it yourself, except perhaps that you get to chat with your co-workers, which could be good if you like them. Mostly though what you're doing in that case is wasting a bunch of people's time instead of just wasting your own time.

> **So don't waste people's time, and don't create more complexity than you need to in your codebase. This debugging method works. It works every time, on every codebase, with every system.**

Sometimes the "data gathering" step is pretty hard, particularly with bugs that you can't reproduce. But at the worst, you can gather data by looking at the code and trying to see if you can *see* a bug in it, or draw a diagram of how the system behaves and see if you can perceive a problem there. I would only recommend that as a last resort, but if you have to, it's still better than guessing what's wrong or assuming you already know.

Sometimes, it's almost magical how a bug resolves just by looking at the right data until you *know*. Try it for yourself and see. It can actually be fun, even.

-Max

— Part Five —

Engineering in Teams

~ 18 ~

EFFECTIVE ENGINEERING PRODUCTIVITY

Often, people who work on engineering productivity either come into conflict with the developers they are attempting to help, or spend a long time working on some project that ends up not mattering because nobody actually cares about it.

This comes about because the problem that you see that a development team has is not necessarily the problem that they know exists. For example, you could come into the team and see that they have hopelessly *complex code* and so they can't write good tests or maintain the system easily. However, the developers aren't really aware that they have complex code or that this complexity is causing the trouble that they are having. What they are aware of is something like, "we can only release once a month and the whole team has to stay at work until 10:00 PM to get the release out on the day that we release."

When engineering productivity workers encounter this situation, some of them just try to ignore the developers' complaints and just go start refactoring code. This doesn't really work, for several reasons. The first is that both management and some other developers will resist you, making it more difficult than it needs to be to get the job done.

But if just simple resistance were the problem, you could overcome it. The real problem is that *you* will become unreal and irrelevant to the company, even if you're doing the best job that anybody's ever seen. Your management will try to dissuade you from doing your job, or even try to get rid of you. When you're already tackling technical complexity, you don't need to also be tackling a whole company that's opposed to you.

In time, many engineering productivity workers develop an adversarial attitude toward the developers that they are working with. They feel that if the engineers would "just use the tool that I wrote" then surely all would be well. But the developers *aren't* using the tool that you wrote, so why does your tool even matter?

The problem here is that when you *start off* ignoring developer complaints (or don't even find out what problems developers think they have) that's *already* inherently adversarial. That is, it's not that everything started off great and then somehow became this big conflict. It actually started off with a conflict, by you thinking that there was one problem, and the developers thinking there was a different problem.

And it's not just that the company will be resistive — this situation is also highly demoralizing to the individual engineering productivity worker. In general, people like to get things *done*. They like for their work to have some *result*, to have some *effect*.

If you do a bunch of refactoring but nobody maintains the code's simplicity, or you write some tool/framework that nobody uses, then ultimately you're not really *doing* anything, and that's disheartening.

So What Should You Do?

So what *should* you do? Well, we've established that if you simply disagree with (or don't know) the problem that developers think they have, then you'll most likely end up frustrated, demoralized, and possibly even out of a job. So what's the solution? Should you just do whatever the developers tell you to do? After all, that would probably make them happy and keep you employed and all that.

Well, yes, you will accomplish that (keeping your job and making some people happy)...well, maybe for a little while. You see, this approach is actually very shortsighted. If the developers you are working with knew exactly how to resolve the situation they are in, it's probable that they would never have gotten themselves into it in the first place.

That isn't always true — sometimes you're working with a new group of people who have taken over an old codebase, but in that case then usually this new group *is* the "productivity worker" that I'm talking about, or maybe you *are* one of these new developers. Or some other situation. But even then, if you only provide the solutions that are suggested to you, you'll end up with the same problems that I describe in *Chapter 40, Users Have Problems, Developers Have Solutions.* That is, when you work in developer productivity, the developers are your users.

You can't just accept any suggestion they have for how you should implement your solutions. It might make some people happy for a little while, but you end up with a system that's not only hard to maintain, it also only represents the needs of the loudest users — who are probably not the majority of your users.

So then you have a poorly-designed system that doesn't even have the features its actual users want, which once again leads to you not getting promoted, being frustrated, etc. Also, there's a particular problem that happens in this space with developer productivity. If you only provide the solutions that developers specify, you usually never get around to resolving the actual underlying problems.

For example, if the developers think the release of their 10-million-lines-of-code monolithic binary is taking too long, and you just spend all your time making the release tools faster, you're never going to get to a *good* state. You might get to a *better* state (somewhat faster releases) but you'll never resolve the *real* problem, which is that the binary is just too damn large.

The Solution

So *what*, then? Not doing what they say means failing, and doing what they say means only mediocre success. Where's the middle ground here?

The correct solution here is similar to what I discuss in *Chapter 40, Users Have Problems, Developers Have Solutions*, but it has a few extra pieces. Using this method, I have not only solved significant underlying problems in vast codebases, I have actually changed the development culture of significant engineering organizations. So it works pretty well, when done correctly.

The first thing to do is to find out what problems the developers think they have. Don't make any judgments. Go around and talk to people. Don't just ask the managers or the senior executives. They usually say something completely different from what the real software engineers say.

Go around and talk to a lot of people who work directly on the codebase. If you can't get everybody, get the technical lead from each team. And then yes, also do talk to the management, because they also have problems that you want to address and you should understand what those are. But if you want to solve *developer* problems, you have to find out what those problems are from *developers*.

There's a trick that I use here during this phase. In general, developers aren't very good at saying where code complexity lies if you just ask them directly. Like, if you just ask, "What is too complex?" or "What do you find difficult?", they will think for a bit and may or may not come up with anything.

But if you ask most developers for an *emotional reaction* to the code that they work on or work with, they will almost *always* have something. I ask questions like, "Is there some part of your job that you find really annoying?" "Is there some piece of code that's always been frustrating to work with?" "Is there some part of the codebase that you're afraid to touch because you think you'll break it?" And to managers, "Is there some part of the codebase that developers are always complaining about?"

You can adjust these questions to your situation, and remember that you want to be having a real conversation with developers — not just robotically reading off a list of questions. They are going to say things that you're going to want more specifics on. You'll probably want to take notes, and so forth.

After a while of doing this, you'll start to get the idea that there is a common theme (or a few common themes) between the complaints. If you've read my other book, *Code Simplicity*, or if you've worked in engineering productivity for a while, you'll usually realize that the real underlying cause of the problems is some sort of code complexity.

But that's not purely the theme we're looking for – we could have figured that out without even talking to anybody. We're looking for something a bit higher level, like "building the binary is slow." There might be several themes that come up.

Now, you'll have a bunch of data, and there are a few things you can do with it. Usually engineering management will be interested in some of this information that you've collected, and presenting it to them will make you real to the managers and hopefully foster some agreement that something needs to be done about the problem. That's not necessary to do as part of this solution, but sometimes you'll want to do it, based on your own judgment of the situation.

Credibility and Solving Problems

The first thing you should do with the data is find some problem that developers *know* they have, that you know you can do something about in a short period of time (like a month or two) and deliver that solution. This doesn't have to be life-changing or completely alter the way that everybody works. In fact, it really should *not* do that. Because the point of this change is to make your work *credible*.

> **When you work in engineering productivity, you live or die by your personal credibility.**

You see, at some point you need to be able to get down to the real problem. And the *only* way that you're going to be able to do that is if the developers find you *credible* enough to believe you and trust you when you want to make some change. So you need to do something at first to become credible to the team.

It's not some huge, all-out change. It's something that you know you can do, even if it's a bit difficult. It helps if it's something that other people have tried to do and failed, because then you also demonstrate that in fact something *can* be done about this mess that other people perhaps failed to handle (and then everybody felt hopeless about the whole thing and just decided they'd have to live with the mess forever, and it can't be fixed and blah blah blah so on and so on).

Once you've established your basic credibility by handling this initial problem, then you can start to look at what problem the developers have and what you think the best solution to that would be. Now, often, this is not something you can implement all at once. And this is another important point – you can't change everything about a team's culture or development process all at once. You have to do it incrementally, deal with the "fallout" of the change (people getting mad because you changed something, or because it's all different now, or because your first iteration of the change doesn't work well) and wait for that to calm down before moving on to the next step.

If you tried to change everything all at once, you'd essentially have a rebellion on your hands – a rebellion that would result in the end of your credibility and the failure of all your efforts. You'd be right back in the same pit that the other two, non-working solutions from above end you up in – being demoralized or ineffective. So you have to work in steps. Some teams can accept larger steps, and some can only accept smaller ones. Usually, the larger the team, the more slowly you have to go.

The Blocker

Now, sometimes at this point you run into somebody who is such a curmudgeon that you just can't seem to make forward progress. Sometimes there is some person who is very senior who is either very set in their ways or just kind of crazy. (You can usually tell the latter because the crazy ones are frequently insulting or rude.) How much progress you can make in this case depends partly on your communication skills, partly on your willingness to persist, but also partly in how you go about resolving this situation.

In general, what you want to do is find your allies and create a core support group for the efforts you are making. Almost always, the majority of developers want sanity to prevail, even if they aren't saying anything.

Just being publicly encouraging when somebody says they want to improve something goes a long way. Don't demand that everybody make the *perfect* change – you're gathering your "team" and validating the idea that code cleanup, productivity improvements, etc. are valuable. And you have something like a volunteer culture or an open-source project – you have to be very encouraging and kind in order to foster its growth. That doesn't mean you should accept bad changes, but if somebody wants to make things better, then you should at least acknowledge them and say that's great.

Sometimes 9 out of 10 people all want to do the right thing, but they are being overruled by the one loud person who they feel they must bow down to or respect beyond rationality, for some reason. So you basically do what you can with the group of people who do support you, and make the progress that you can make that way. Usually, it's actually even possible to ignore the one loud person and just get on with making things better anyway.

If you ultimately get totally stopped by some senior person, then either (a) you didn't go about this the right way (meaning that you didn't follow my recommendations above, there's some communication difficulty, you're genuinely trying to do something that would be bad for developers, etc.) or (b) the person stopping you is outright insane, no matter how "normal" they seem.

If you're blocked because you're doing the wrong thing, then figure out what would help developers the most and do that instead. Sometimes this is as simple as doing a better job of communicating with the person who's blocking you.

Like, for example, stop being adversarial or argumentative, but listen to what they person has to say and see if you can work with them. Being kind, interested, and helpful goes a long way. But if it's not that, and you're being stopped by a crazy person, and you can't make *any* progress even with your supporters, then you should probably find another team to work with.

It's not worth *your* sanity and happiness to go up against somebody who will never listen to reason and who is dead set on stopping you at all costs. Go somewhere where you can make a difference in the world rather than hitting your head up against a brick wall forever.

That's not everything there is to know about handling that sort of situation with a person who's blocking your work, but it gives you the basics. Persist, be kind, form a group of your supporters, don't do things that would cause you to lose credibility, and find the things that you *can* do to help. Usually the resistance will crumble slowly over time, or the people who don't like things getting better will leave.

Moving Towards the Fundamental Problem

So let's say that you are making progress improving productivity by incremental steps, and you are in some control over any situations that might stop you. Where do you go from there? Well, make sure that you're moving towards the *fundamental* problem with your incremental steps.

At some point, you need to start changing the way that people write software in order to solve the problem. There is a lot to know about this, which I've either written up before or I'll write up later. But at some point you're going to need to get down to simplifying code. When do you get to do that? Usually, when you've incrementally gotten to the point where there is a problem that you can credibly indicate refactoring as part of the solution to.

Don't promise the world, and don't say that you're going to start making a graph of improved developer productivity from the refactoring work that you are going to do. Managers (and some developers) will want various things from you, sometimes unreasonable demands born out of a lack of understanding of what you do (or sometimes from the outright desire to block you by placing unreasonable requirements on your work). No, you have to have some problem where you can say "Hey, it would be nice to refactor this piece of code so that we can write feature X more easily," or something like that.

From there, you keep proposing refactorings where you can. This doesn't mean that you stop working on tooling, testing, process, etc. But your persistence on *refactoring* is what changes the culture the most. What you want is for people to think "we always clean up code when we work on things," or "code quality is important," or whatever it takes to get the culture that you want.

Once you have a culture where things are getting *better* rather than getting worse, the problem will tend to eventually fix itself over time, even if you don't work on it anymore. This doesn't mean you should stop at this point, but at the worst, once everybody cares about code quality, testing, productivity, etc. you'll see things start to resolve themselves without you having to be actively involved.

Remember, this whole process isn't about "building consensus." You're not going for total agreement from everybody in the group about how *you* should do *your* job. It's about finding out what people *know* is broken and giving them solutions to that, solutions that they can accept and which improve your credibility with the team, but also solutions which incrementally work toward resolving the real underlying problems of the codebase, not just pandering to whatever developer need happens to be the loudest at the moment. If you had to keep only one thing in mind, it's:

> **Solve the problems that people know they have, not the problems *you* think they have.**

One last thing that I'll point out, is that I've talked a lot about this as though you were personally responsible for the engineering productivity of a whole company or a whole team. That's not always the case – in fact, it's probably not the case for most people who work in engineering productivity. Some people work on a smaller part of a tool, a framework, a sub-team, etc.

This point about solving the problems that are *real* still applies. Actually, probably most of what I wrote above can be adapted to this particular case, but the *most* important thing is that you *not* go off and solve the problem that you think developers have, but that instead you solve a problem that (a) you can prove exists and (b) that the developers know exists.

Many of the engineering productivity teams that I've worked with have violated this so badly that they have spent years writing tools or frameworks that developers didn't want, never used, and which the developers actually worked to *delete* when the person who designed them was gone. What a pointless waste of time! So don't waste your time. Be effective. And change the world.

-Max

~ 19 ~

MEASURING DEVELOPER PRODUCTIVITY

Almost as long as I have been working to make the lives of software engineers better, people have been asking me how to measure developer productivity. How do we tell where there are productivity problems? How do we know if a team is doing worse or better over time? How does a manager explain to senior managers how productive the developers are? And so on and so on.

In general, I tended to focus on code simplicity first, and put a lower priority on measuring every single thing that developers do. Almost all software problems can be traced back to some failure to apply software engineering principles and practices. So even without measurements, if you simply get good software engineering practices applied across a company, most productivity problems and development issues disappear.

Now that said, there is tremendous value in measuring things. It helps you pinpoint areas of difficulty, allows you to reward those whose productivity improves, justifies spending more time on developer productivity work where that is necessary, and has many other advantages.

But programming is not like other professions. You can't measure it like you would measure some manufacturing process, where you could just count the number of correctly-made items rolling off the assembly line. So how *would* you measure the production of a programmer?

The Definition of "Productivity"

The secret is in appropriately defining the word "productivity." Many people say that they want to "measure productivity," but have never thought about what *productivity* actually *is*. How can you measure something if you haven't even defined it?

The key to understanding what productivity is, is realizing that it has to do with *products*. A person who is productive is a person who regularly and efficiently produces *products*.

> **The way to measure the productivity of a developer is to measure the product that they produce.**

That statement alone probably isn't enough to resolve the problem, though. So let me give you some examples of things you *wouldn't* measure, and then some things you would, to give you a general idea.

Why Not "Lines of Code?"

Probably the most common metrics that the software industry has attempted to develop have been centered around how many lines of code (abbreviated LoC) a developer writes. I understand why people have tried to do this — it seems to be something that you can measure, so why not keep track of it? A *coder* who writes more *code* is more productive, right? Well, no. Part of the trick here is:

> ## "Computer programmer" is not actually a job.

Wait, what? But I see ads all over the place for "programmer" as a job! Well, yes, but you also see ads for "carpenter" all over the place. But what does "a carpenter" produce? Unless you get more specific, it's hard to say. You might say that a carpenter makes "cut pieces of wood," but that's not a product — nobody's going to hire you to pointlessly cut or shape pieces of wood.

So what would be a *job* that "a carpenter" could do? Well, the *job* might be furniture repair, or building houses, or making tables. In each case, the carpenter's product is different. If he's a Furniture Repairman (a valid job) then you would measure how much furniture he repaired well. If he was building houses, you might measure how many rooms he completed that didn't have any carpentry defects.

The point here is this:

> ## "Computer programmer," like "carpenter," is a *skill*, not a *job*.

You don't measure the practice of a skill if you want to know how much a person is producing. You measure something about the *product* that that skill produces. To take this to an absurd level – just to illustrate the point – part of the skill of computer programming these days involves typing on a keyboard, but would you measure a programmer's productivity by how many keys they hit on the keyboard per day? Obviously not.

Measuring lines of code is less absurd than measuring keys hit on a keyboard, because it does seem like one of the things a programmer produces – a line of code *seems* like a finished thing that can be delivered, even if it's small.

But is it really a *product*, all by itself? If I estimated a job as taking 1000 lines of code, and I was going to charge $1000 for it, would my client pay me $1 if I only delivered one line of code? No, my client would pay me nothing, because I didn't deliver any product at all.

So how would you apply this principle in the real world to correctly measure the production of a programmer?

Determining a Valid Metric

The first thing to figure out is: what is the program producing that is of value to its users? Usually this is answered by a fast look at the chapter *The Purpose of Software* from *Code Simplicity*, which talks about how the purpose of software is "to help people." So the first step here would be to determine what group of people you're helping do what with your software, and then figure out how you would describe the result of that help as a product.

For example, if you have accounting software that helps individuals file their taxes, you might measure the total number of tax returns fully and correctly filed by individuals using your software. Yes, other people contribute to that too (such as salespeople) but the programmer is primarily responsible for how easily and successfully the actual work gets done.

One might want to pick metrics that focus closely on things that only the programmer has control over, but don't go overboard on that – the programmer doesn't have to be the *only* person who could possibly influence a metric in order for it to be a valid measurement of their personal production.

There could be multiple things to measure for one system, too. Let's say you're working on a shopping website. A backend developer of that website might measure something about the number of data requests successfully filled, whereas a frontend developer of a shopping cart for the site might measure how many items are put into carts successfully, how many people get through the checkout flow successfully every day, etc.

Of course, one would also make sure that any metric proposed also aligns with the overall metric(s) of the whole system. For example, if a backend developer is just measuring "number of data requests received at the backend" but not caring if they are correctly filled, how quickly they are filled, or whatever, they could design a poor API that requires too many calls and that actually harms the overall user experience.

So you have to make sure that any metric you're looking at, you compare it to the reality of helping your actual users. In this particular case, a better solution might be to count, say, how many "submit payment" requests are processed correctly, since that's the end result. (I wouldn't take that as the only possible metric for the backend of a shopping website, by the way – that's just one possible thought.)

What About When Your Product Is Code?

There *are* people who deliver code as their product. For example, a library developer's product *is* code. But it's rarely a single line of code – it's more like an entire function, class, or set of classes. You might measure something like "Number of fully-tested public API functions released for use by programmers" for a library developer.

You'd probably have to do something to count new features for existing functions in that case, too, like counting every new feature for a function that improves its API as being a whole new "function" delivered. Of course, since the original metric says "fully tested," any new feature would have to be fully tested as well, to count.

But however you choose to measure it, the point here is that even for the small number of people whose product is code, you're measuring the *product*.

What about People Who Work on Developer Productivity?

That does leave one last category, which is people who work on improving developer productivity. If it's your job to help other developers move more quickly, how do you measure that?

Well, first off, most people who work on developer productivity *do* have some specific product. Either they work on a test framework (which you would measure in a similar fashion to how you would measure a library) or they work on some tool that developers use, in which case you would measure something about the success or usage of that tool.

For example, one thing the developers of a bug tracking system might want to measure is number of bugs successfully and rapidly resolved. Of course, you would modify that to take into account how the tool was being used in the company – maybe some entries in the bug tracker are intended to live for a long time, so you would measure those entries some other way. In general, you'd ask: what is the *product* or *result* that we bring about in the world by working on this tool? So that's what you'd measure – the product.

But what if you don't work on some specific framework or tool? In that case, perhaps your product has something to do with *software engineers* themselves. Maybe you would measure the number of times an engineer was assisted by your work. Or the amount of engineering time saved by your changes, if you can reliably measure that (which is rarely possible). In general, though, this work can be much trickier to measure than other types of programming.

One thing that I have proposed in the past (though have not actually attempted to do yet) is, if you have a person who helps particular teams with productivity, measure the *improvement* in productivity that those teams experience over time. Or perhaps measure the rate at which the team's metrics improve.

For example, let's say that we are measuring a product purely in terms of how much money it brings in. (Note: it would be rare to measure a product *purely* by this metric – this is an artificial example to demonstrate how this all works.)

Let's say in the first week the product brought in $100. Next week $101, and next week $102. That's an increase, so it's not that bad, but it's not that exciting. Then Mary comes along and helps the team with productivity. The product makes $150 that week, then $200, then $350 as Mary continues to work on it.

It's gone from increasing at a rate of $1 a week to increasing at a rate of $50, then $100, then $150 a week. That seems like a valid thing to measure for Mary. Of course, there could be other things that contribute to that metric improving, so it's not perfect, but it's better than nothing if you really do have a "pure" productivity developer.

Conclusion

There are lots of other things to know about how to measure production of employees, teams, and companies in general. The above points are only intended to discuss how to take a programmer and figure out what general sort of thing you should be measuring.

There's a lot more to know about the right way to do measurements, how to interpret those measurements, and how to choose metrics that don't suck.

Hopefully, though, the above should get you started on solving the great mystery of how to measure the production of individual programmers, teams, and whole software organizations.

-Max

∼ 20 ∼

How to Handle Code Complexity in a Software Company

Here's an obvious statement that has some subtle consequences:

> **Only an individual programmer can resolve code complexity.**

That is, resolving code complexity requires the attention of an individual person on that code. They can certainly use appropriate tools to make the task easier, but ultimately it's the application of human intelligence, attention, and work that simplifies code. So what? Why does this matter? Well, to be clearer:

> **Resolving code complexity usually requires detailed work at the level of the individual contributor.**

If a manager just says "simplify the code!" and leaves it at that, usually nothing happens because,

a.   they're not being specific enough,

b.   they don't necessarily have the knowledge required about each individual piece of code in order to *be* that specific, and

c.   part of understanding the problem is actually going through the process of solving it, and the manager isn't the person writing the solution.

The higher a manager's level in the company, the more true this is. When a CTO, Vice President, or Engineering Director gives an instruction like "improve code quality" but doesn't get much more specific than that, what tends to happen is that a lot of *motion* occurs in the company but the codebase doesn't significantly improve.

It's very tempting, if you're a software engineering manager, to propose broad, sweeping solutions to problems that affect large areas. The problem with that approach to *code complexity* is that the problem is usually composed of many different small projects that require detailed work from individual programmers.

So, if you try to handle everything with the same broad solution, that solution won't fit most of the situations that need to be handled. Your attempt at a broad solution will actually backfire, with software engineers feeling like they did a lot of work but didn't actually produce a maintainable, simple codebase.

> **This is a common pattern in software management, and it contributes to the mistaken belief that code complexity is inevitable and nothing can be done about it.**

So what *can* you do as a manager, if you have a complex codebase and want to resolve it? Well, the trick is to get the data from the individual contributors and then work with them to help them resolve the issues. In this chapter we'll look in detail at how this sequence unfolds usually in six steps.

Step 1 – Problem Lists

Ask each member of your team to write down a list of what frustrates them about the code. The symptoms of code complexity are things like emotional reactions to code, confusions about code, feeling like a piece will break if you touch it, difficulties optimizing, etc. So you want the answers to questions like, "Is there a part of the system that makes you nervous when you modify it?" or "Is there some part of the codebase that frustrates you to work with?"

Each individual software engineer should write their own list. I wouldn't recommend implementing some system for collecting the lists – just have people write down the issues for themselves in whatever way is easiest for them. Give them a few days to write this list; they might think of other things over time.

The list doesn't just have to be about your own codebase, but can be about any code that the developer has to work with or use. You're looking for symptoms at this point, not causes. Developers can be as general or as specific as they want, for this list.

Step 2 – Meeting

Call a meeting with your team and have each person bring their list and a computer that they can use to access the codebase. The ideal size for a team meeting like this is about six or seven people, so you might want to break things down into sub-teams.

In this meeting you want to go over the lists and get **the name of a specific directory, file, class, method, or block of code** to associate with each symptom.

Even if somebody says something like,

> **"The whole codebase has no unit tests,"**

then you might say,

> **"Tell me about a specific time that that affected you,"**

and use the response to that to narrow down what files it's most important to write unit tests for right away.

You also want to be sure that you're really getting a description of the *problem*, which might be something more like "It's difficult to refactor the codebase because I don't know if I'm breaking other people's modules." Then unit tests might be the *solution*, but you first want to narrow down specifically where the *problem* lies, as much as possible. (It's true that almost all code should be unit tested, but if you don't have *any* unit tests, you'll need to start off with some doable task on the subject.)

In general, the idea here is that only *code* can actually be fixed, so you have to know what piece of code is the problem. It might be true that there's a broad problem, but that problem can be broken down into specific problems with specific pieces of code that are affected, one by one.

Step 3 – Bug Reports

Using the information from the meeting, file a bug describing the problem (not the solution, just the problem!) for each directory, file, class, etc. that was named. A bug could be something as simple as "FrobberFactory is hard to understand."

If a solution was suggested during the meeting, you can note that in the bug, but the bug itself should primarily be about the problem.

Step 4 – Prioritization

Now it's time to prioritize. The first thing to do is to look at which issues affect the largest number of developers the most severely. Those are high priority issues. Usually this part of prioritization is done by somebody who has a broad view over developers in the team or company. Often, this is a manager.

That said, sometimes issues have an order that they should be resolved in that is not directly related to their severity. For example, Issue X has to be resolved before Issue Y can be resolved, or resolving Issue A would make resolving Issue B easier.

This means that Issue A and Issue X should be fixed first even if they're not as severe as the issues that they block. Often, there's a chain of issues like this and the trick is to find the issue at the bottom of the stack.

Handling this part of prioritization incorrectly is one of the most common and major mistakes in software design. It may seem like a minor detail, but in fact it is critical to the success of efforts to resolve complexity.

> **The essence of good software design in *all* situations is *taking the right actions in the right sequence*.**
>
> **Forcing developers to tackle issues out of sequence (without regard for which problems underlie which other problems) will cause code complexity.**

This part of prioritization is a technical task that is usually best done by the technical lead of the team. Sometimes this is a manager, but other times it's a senior software engineer.

Sometimes you don't really know which issue to tackle first until you're doing development on one piece of code and you discover that it would be easier to fix a different piece of code first. With that said, if you can determine the ordering up front, it's good to do so. But if you find that you'd have to get into actually figuring out solutions in order to determine the ordering, just skip it for now.

Whether you do it up front or during development, it's important that individual programmers *do* realize when there is an underlying task to tackle before the one they have been assigned. They must be empowered to switch from their current task to the one that actually blocks them.

There is a limit to this (for example, rewriting the whole system into another language just to fix one file is not a good use of time) but generally, "finding the issue at the bottom of the stack" is one of the most important tasks a developer has when doing these sorts of cleanups.

Step 5 – Assignment

Now you assign each bug to an individual contributor. This is a pretty standard managerial process, and while it definitely involves some detailed work and communication, I would imagine that most software engineering managers are already familiar with how to do it.

One tricky piece here is that some of the bugs might be about code that isn't maintained by your team. In that case you'll have to work appropriately through the organization to get the appropriate team to take responsibility for the issue. It helps to have buy-in from a manager that you have in common with the other team, higher up the chain, here.

In some organizations, if the other team's problem is not too complex or detailed, it might also be possible for your team to just make the changes themselves. This is a judgment call that you can make based on what you think is best for overall productivity.

Step 6 – Planning

Now that you have all of these bugs filed, you have to figure out *when* to address them. Generally, the right thing to do is to make sure that developers regularly fix some of the code quality issues that you filed along with their feature work.

If your team makes plans for a period of time like a quarter or six weeks, you should include some of the code cleanups in every plan. The best way to do this is to have developers first do cleanups that would make their specific feature work easier, and then have them do that feature work.

Usually this doesn't even slow down their feature work overall. (That is, if this is done correctly, developers can usually accomplish the same amount of feature work in a quarter that they could even if they *weren't* also doing code cleanups, providing evidence that the code cleanups are already improving productivity.)

Don't stop normal feature development entirely to just work on code quality. Instead, make sure that enough code quality work is being done continuously that the quality of the codebase is always improving *overall* rather than getting worse over time.

If you do those things, that should get you well on the road to an actually-improving codebase. There's actually quite a bit to know about this process in general – perhaps enough for another entire book. However, the above plus some common sense and experience should be enough to make major improvements in the quality of your codebase, and perhaps even improve your life as a software engineer or manager, too.

-Max

~ 21 ~

REFACTORING IS ABOUT FEATURES

When you clean up code, you are always doing it in the service of the product. Refactoring is essentially an *organizational* process (not the definition of "organizational" meaning "having to do with a business" but the definition meaning "having to do with putting things in order"). That is, you're putting in order so that you can do something.

When you start refactoring for the sake of refactoring alone, refactoring gets a bad name. People start to think that you're wasting your time, you lose your credibility, and your manager or peers will stop you from continuing your work.

When I say "refactoring for the sake of refactoring alone," what I mean is looking at a piece of code that has *nothing* to do with what you're actually working on, saying, "I don't like the way that this is designed," and moving parts of the design around without affecting the functionality of the system.

This is like watering the lawn when your house is on fire. If your codebase is like most of the codebases I've seen, "your house is on fire" is probably even an appropriate analogy. Even so, if things aren't that bad, the point is that you're focusing on something that doesn't need to be focused on.

You might feel like you're doing a great job of reorganizing the code, and probably you are, but the *point* of watering your lawn is to have a nice lawn *in front of your house*. If your refactoring has nothing to do with the current product or feature goals of your system, you're not actually accomplishing anything other than re-ordering something that nobody is using, involved with, or cares about.

Being Effective

So what is it that you want to do? Well, usually, what you want to do is pick a feature that you want to get implemented, and figure out what you could refactor that would make it easier to implement that. Or you find an area of the code that is frequently being worked on and get some reorganization done in that area. This will make people *appreciate* your work. It's not just about that — it's really about the fact that they will appreciate it because you are doing something *effective*. But getting appreciation for the work that you've done — or at least some form of polite acknowledgment — can help encourage you to continue, can show you that other people are starting to care about your work, and hopefully help spread good development practices across your company.

Is there ever a time when you would tackle a refactoring project that doesn't have something *directly* to do with the work that you have to do? Well, sometimes you would refactor something that has to do *indirectly* with the goal that you have.

Sometimes when you start looking at a particularly complex problem, it's like trying to pick up rocks on the beach to get down to the sand at the bottom. You try to move a rock, and figure out that first, you have to move some other rock. Then you discover that that rock is up against a large boulder, and there are rocks all around *that* boulder that prevent it from being moved, and so forth.

So within reason, you have to handle the issues that are blocking you from doing refactoring. If these problems get large enough, you will need a dedicated engineer whose job it is to resolve these problems — in particular the problems that block refactoring itself. (For example, maybe the dependencies of your code or its build system are so complex that nobody can move any code anywhere, and if that's a big enough problem, it could be months of work for one person.)

Of course, ideally you'd never get into a situation where your problems are so big that they can't be moved by an individual doing their normal job. The way that you accomplish that is by following the principles of incremental development and design as discussed in *Code Simplicity*. Essentially, this means you should always make the system look like it was designed to do the job that it's doing now.

But assuming that you are like most of the software projects in the world who *didn't* do that, you're now in some sort of bad situation and need to be dug out of the pile of rocks that your system has buried itself under. I wouldn't feel bad about this, mostly because feeling bad about it doesn't really accomplish anything.

Instead of feeling bad about it or feeling confused about it, what you need to do is to have some sort of system that will let you attack the problem incrementally and get to a better state from where you are. This is a lot more complex than keeping the system well-designed as you go, but it can be done.

The key principle to cleaning up a complex codebase is to always refactor in the service of a feature.

See, the problem is that you have this mountain of "rocks." You have something like a house on fire, except that the house is the size of several mountains and it's all on fire all the time. You need to figure out which part of the "mountain" or "house" that you actually need right now, and get that into good shape so that it can be "used," on a series of small steps.

This isn't a perfect analogy, since a fire is temporary, dangerous, and life-threatening. It will also destroy things faster than you can clean them up. But sometimes a codebase is actually in that state — it's getting worse faster than it's getting better. That's another principle:

> **Your first goal is to get the system into a place where it's getting better over time, instead of getting worse.**

These are practically the *same* principle, even though they sound completely different. How can that be? Because the way that you get the codebase to get better over time instead of getting worse is that you get people to refactor the code that they are about to add features to right before they add features to it.

You look at a piece of code. Let's say that it's a piece of code that generates a list of employee names at your company. You have to add a new feature to sort the list by the date they were hired. You're reading the code, and you can't figure out what the variable names mean.

So the first thing you'd do, before adding the new feature, is to make a *separate*, self-contained change that improves the variable names. After you do that, you still can't understand the code, because it's all in one function that contains 1000 lines of code. So you split it up into several functions.

Maybe now it's good enough, and you feel like it would be pretty simple to add the new sorting feature. Maybe you want to change those functions into well-designed objects before you continue, though, if you're in an object-oriented language. It's all sort of up to you – the basic point is that you should be making things *better* and they should be getting better faster than they're getting worse. It's a judgment point as to how far you go.

You have to balance the fact that you *do* need to make forward progress on your feature goals, and that you can't just refactor your code forever.

Setting Refactoring Boundaries

In general, I set some boundary around my code, like "I'm not going to refactor anything outside of my project to get this feature done," or "I'm not going to wait for a change to the programming language itself before I can release this feature."

But within my boundary, I try to do a good job. And I try to set the boundary as wide as possible without getting into a situation where I won't be able to actually develop my feature. Usually that's a time boundary as well as a "scope of codebase" (like, how far outside of my codebase) boundary – the time part is often the most important, like "I'm not going to do a three-month project to develop a two-day feature."

But even with that I balance things on the side of spending time on the refactoring, especially when I first start doing this in a codebase and it's a new thing and the whole thing is very messy.

Refactoring Doesn't Waste Time, It Saves It

And that brings us to another point – even though you might think that it's going to take more time to refactor and then develop your feature, in my experience it usually takes less time or the same amount of time overall. "Overall" here includes all the time that you would spend debugging, rolling back releases, sending out bug fixes, writing tests for complex systems, etc.

It might seem faster to write a feature in your complex system without refactoring, and sometimes it is, but most of the time you'll spend less time *overall* if you do a good job of putting the system in order first before you start adding new feature. This isn't just theoretical – I've demonstrated it to be the case many times.

I've actually had my team finish projects *faster* than teams who were working on newer codebases with better tools when we did this. (That is, the other team should have been able to out-develop us, but we refactored continuously in the service of the product, and always got our releases out faster and were actually ahead in terms of features, with roughly the same number of developers on both projects working on very similar features.)

Refactoring To Clarity

There's another point that I use to decide when I'm "done" with refactoring a particular piece of code, which is that I think that other people will be able to clearly see the pattern I've designed and will maintain the code *in that pattern* from then on.

Sometimes I have to write a little piece of documentation that describes the intended design of the system, so that people will follow it, but in general my theory (and this one really is just a theory – I don't have enough evidence for it yet) is that if I design a piece of code well enough, it shouldn't need a piece of documentation describing how it's supposed to be designed. It should probably be visible just from reading the code how it's designed, and it should be *so obvious* how you'd add a new feature within that design that nobody would ever do it otherwise. Obviously, *perfectly* achieving that goal would be impossible, but that's a general truth in software design:

> **There is no perfect design, there is only a *better* design.**

So that's another way that you know that you're "bikeshedding" or over-engineering or spending too much time on figuring out how to refactor something – that you're trying to make it "perfect." It's not going to be "perfect," because there is no "perfect." There's "does a good job for the purpose that it has." That is, you can't even really judge whether or not a design *is* good without understanding the purpose the code is being designed for. One design would be good for one purpose, another design would be good for another purpose.

Yes, there are generic libraries, but even that is a purpose. And the best generic libraries are designed by actual experimentation with real codebases where you can verify that they serve specific purposes very well.

> **When you're refactoring, the idea is to change the design from one that doesn't currently suit the purpose well to a design that fits the current purpose that piece of code has.**

That's not all there is to know about refactoring, but it's a pretty good basic principle to start with.

Summary

So, in brief, refactoring is an organizational process that you go through in order to make production possible. If you aren't going toward production when you refactor, you're going to run into *lots* of different kinds of trouble. I can't even tell you all of the things that are going to go wrong, but they're going to happen. On the other hand, if you just try to produce a system and you never reorganize it, you're going to get yourself into such a mess that production becomes difficult or impossible.

So both of these things have to be done — you must produce a product, and you must organize the system in such a way that the product can be produced quickly, reliably, simply, and well. If you leave out organization, you won't get the product that you want, and if you leave out production, then there's literally no reason to even be doing the refactoring in the first place.

Yes, it's nice to water the lawn, but let's put out some fires, first.

-Max

~ 22 ~

KINDNESS
AND CODE

It is very easy to think of software development as being an entirely technical activity, where humans don't really matter and everything is about the computer. However, the opposite is actually true.

> **Software engineering is fundamentally a human discipline.**

Many of the mistakes made over the years in trying to fix software development have been made by focusing purely on the technical aspects of the system without thinking about the fact that it is human beings who write the code. When you see somebody who cares about optimization more than readability of code; when you see somebody who won't write a comment but will spend all day tweaking their shell scripts to be fewer lines, when you have somebody who can't communicate but worships small binaries: then you're seeing various symptoms of this problem.

Software is about People

In reality, software systems are written by people. They are read by people, modified by people, understood or not by people. They represent the mind of the developers that wrote them. They are the closest thing to a raw representation of thought that we have on Earth. They are not themselves human, alive, intelligent, emotional, evil, or good.

It's people that have those qualities. Software is used entirely and only to serve people. Software is the product of people, and it is usually the product of a group of those people who had to work together, communicate, understand each other, and collaborate effectively. As such, there's an important point to be made about working with a group of software engineers:

> **There is no value to being cruel to other people in the development community.**

It doesn't help to be rude to the people that you work with. It doesn't help to angrily tell them that they are wrong and that they shouldn't be doing what they are doing. It does help to make sure that the laws of software design are applied, and that people follow a good path in terms of making systems that can be easily read, understood, and maintained. It doesn't require that you be cruel to do this, though. Sometimes you do have to tell people that they haven't done the right thing. But you can just be matter of fact about it – you don't have to get up in their face or attack them personally for it.

An Example of Kindness

Let's say, for example, that somebody has written a bad piece of code. You have two ways you could comment on this:

"I can't believe you think this is a good idea. Have you ever read a book on software design? Obviously you don't do this."

That's the rude way – it's an attack on the person themselves. Another way you could tell them what's wrong is this:

"This line of code is hard to understand, and this looks like code duplication. Can you refactor this so that it's clearer?"

> **In some ways, the key point here is that you're commenting on the code, and not on the developer.**

But also, the key point is that you're not being a jerk. I mean, come on. The first response is obviously rude. Does it make the person want to work with you, want to contribute more code, or want to get better? No. The second response, on the other hand, lets the person know that they're taking a bad path and that you're not going to let that bad code into the codebase.

The whole reason that you're preventing that programmer from submitting bad code has to do with people in the first place. Either it's about your users or it's about the other developers who will have to read the system. Usually, it's about both, since making a more maintainable system is done entirely so that you can keep on helping users effectively. But one way or another, your work as a software engineer has to do with people.

Yes, a lot of people are going to read the code and use the program, and the person whose code you're reviewing is just one person. So it's possible to think that you can sacrifice some kindness in the name of making this system good for everybody...to look after the many? Maybe you're right. But why be rude or cruel when you don't have to be? Why create that environment on your team that makes people scared of doing the wrong thing, instead of making them happy for doing the right thing?

This extends beyond just code reviews, too. Other software engineers have things to say. You should listen to them, whether you agree or not. Acknowledge their statements politely. Communicate your ideas to them in some constructive fashion.

And look, sometimes people do get angry. Be understanding. Sometimes you're going to get angry too, and you'd probably like your teammates to be understanding when you do.

Be Kind, and Make Better Software

This might all sound kind of airy-fairy, like some sort of unimportant psychobabble. But look. I'm not saying, "Everybody is always right! You should agree with everybody all the time! Don't ever tell anybody that they are wrong! Nobody ever does anything bad!" No, people are frequently wrong, and there are many bad things in the world, and in software engineering, that you have to say no to.

The world is not a good place, always. It's full of stupid people. Some of those stupid people are your co-workers. But even so, you're not going to be doing anything effective by being rude to those stupid people. They don't need your hatred — they need your compassion and your assistance.

And most of your co-workers are probably not stupid people. They are probably intelligent, well-meaning individuals who sometimes make mistakes, just like you do. Give them the benefit of the doubt. Work with them, be kind, and make better software as a result.

-Max

~ 23 ~

OPEN SOURCE COMMUNITY, SIMPLIFIED

Growing and maintaining an open-source community depends essentially on three things:

1. Getting people interested in contributing

2. Removing the barriers to entering the project and contributing

3. Retaining contributors so that they keep contributing

If you can get people interested, then have them actually contribute, and then have them stick around, you have a community. Otherwise, you don't.

If you are just starting a project or need to improve the community of an existing project, you should address these points in reverse order. If you get people interested in a project before you do the later two steps, then people won't be able to enter and won't stick around when they do enter. You won't actually expand your community.

So first, we want to be sure that we can retain both existing and new contributors. Once we've done that, then we want to remove the barriers to entry, so that interested people can actually start contributing. Only *then* do we start worrying about getting people interested.

So let's talk about how you accomplish each step in reverse order.

Retaining Contributors

For the Bugzilla Project (`https://www.bugzilla.org/`), where I helped organize the open-source community, this was our biggest challenge. Once somebody started contributing, what made them keep contributing? How did we keep people around?

Well, we had an interesting advantage in answering these questions, in that we were one of the older open-source projects in existence, having been around since late 1998. So we had a tremendous wealth of actual data to work with.

We mined this data in two ways: First, we did a survey of all our past developers who had left the project, asking them why they had left. This was just a free-form survey, allowing people to answer any way they wanted. Then, we created a graph of the number of contributors over time, for the whole ten years of the project, and correlated the rise and fall of the graphs to various actions we took or didn't take over time.

Once all this was done, I sent an email that out to the developers Bugzilla Project, describing the results of the research. You can read the whole email if you'd like, but I'll summarize the findings here.

1. Don't freeze the trunk for long periods

The Bugzilla Project has a fairly-standard system of having stable branches that receive little change (for example, the "3.4" branch where we commit bug fixes and do minor releases like 3.4.1, 3.4.2, etc.), and a main-line "trunk" repository where all new features go, and which eventually becomes our next *major* release.

In the past, before a major release, we would "freeze" the trunk. This meant that no new features could be developed for several weeks or months until we felt that trunk was stable enough to call a "release candidate." Then we would create a new stable branch from the trunk and re-open the main-line trunk for features. However, while trunk was frozen, there was no feature development happening *anywhere* in the Bugzilla Project.

Graph analysis showed *very clearly* that every time we would freeze, the community would shrink drastically and it would take *several months* after we un-froze for the size of the community to recover. It happened uniformly, every single time we would freeze, over many years and many releases.

Traditional wisdom in open-source is that people like to work on features and don't like to fix bugs. I wouldn't say that that's *exactly* true, but I would say that if you *only* let people fix bugs, then most of them won't stay around.

We addressed this issue by never freezing the trunk. Instead, we branch immediately at the point that we normally would have "frozen" the trunk. The trunk *always* stays open for new feature development.

Yes, this means that for a while, our attention becomes split between the trunk and the latest branch. We're committing the same bug fixes to the branch and the trunk. We are also doing feature development on the trunk simultaneously with those bug fixes. However, we've found that not only does the community expand more rapidly this way, but we also actually get our releases out *more quickly* than we used to. So it's a win-win situation.

2.   Turnover is inevitable

The survey found that the number one reason that contributors leave is that they no longer have time to contribute, or that they were contributing as part of their job and now they have changed jobs. Essentially, it is inevitable that most contributors eventually leave.

So if it community members are definitely going to be leaving, the only way to consistently expand the community is to figure out how to retain **new** contributors. If you don't get new members to stick around, then the community will continuously shrink as old contributors leave, no matter what else you do.

So while retaining existing contributors is important – after all, you want people to stick around and contribute for as long as reasonably possible – what matters the most is retaining new contributors. How do you do that? Well, that's a lot of what the rest of these points are about.

3. Respond to contributions immediately

The Bugzilla Project has a system of code reviews that requires that all new contributions be reviewed by an experienced developer before they can become part of Bugzilla. There have been various complaints about the system over the years, but analyzing the survey data showed that people leave the project because getting a review takes *too long*, not because the reviews are too *hard*. In fact, the reviews can be as hard as you want as long as they happen almost *instantly* after somebody submits a contribution.

People don't (usually) mind having to revise a contribution. They even generally don't mind revising it several times. But they *do* mind if they post a patch, don't get a review for three months, and *then* they have to revise it, only to wait another three months to be told that they have to revise it again. It's the delay that matters, not the level of quality control.

There are other ways of responding rapidly to contributions, too. For example, immediately thanking somebody for posting a patch can go a long way toward retaining new contributors and "converting" them into long-term developers.

4. Be extremely kind and visibly appreciative

For nearly every person who responded to our survey, the factors involved in not staying – beyond "my job changed" or "I didn't have time" – were surprisingly personal.

I know that we all work with computers, and perhaps we'd like to think that engineering should be a totally cold scientific profession where we all do our jobs correctly according to the requirements of the machine, and not worry about our emotional or personal involvements. However, nothing could be further from the truth – the personal interactions that people have with community members, the amount they feel appreciated, and the amount they feel assaulted, are actually the **most important aspects of retaining community members**.

When people contribute on a volunteer basis, they aren't getting paid in money, they are getting paid in admiration, appreciation, the sense of a job well done, and the knowledge that they are helping create a product that affects millions of people. When somebody has contributed a patch, **you need to thank them**. It doesn't matter if the patch is total crap and has to be re-written entirely, **you need to thank them**. They have put some work into this, and if you don't appreciate that, **they will leave before they even start**.

After all, most people get little enough appreciation at their workplace – they stay there because they get paid in money! They don't need to work *for free* with some other organization if it also doesn't appreciate their work, or even worse, assaults every aspect of their contribution before even thanking them for it.

Of course, you still need to correct people on the faults in their contributions. "Kindness" does not include putting bad code into your system. That isn't kind to anybody, including the contributor whose skills probably need to improve, and who may go on believing that something they did in error was in fact correct. You have to still be careful reviewers and very good coders.

What this *does* mean is that in addition to telling people what's *wrong* with their contribution, it's important to appreciate what's *right* about their contribution, even if it's simply the fact that they took the time to contribute. And you have to **actually tell the contributor that you appreciate the contribution**. The more frequently and genuinely that you do this, the more likely you are to retain the contributor.

5. Avoid personal negativity

One thing that drives people away from a project with lightning speed is when they get personally attacked for attempting to do something positive. A "personal attack" can be as little as an unpleasant joke about their code, instead of just a straightforward technical description of what is wrong. Saying something like, "What is wrong with you?" instead of actually leaving some helpful comment. Disguising personal criticism as "an attempt to help them code better" or "help them get along with others." No matter how well-justified these actions may seem to be, they are all personal attacks that are extremely dangerous to your community.

Now truthfully, coding and working on a collaborative project with people who have different viewpoints can get really frustrating sometimes, and I've been an offender in this area just as much as anybody has been. But we all have to learn that it's not okay to insult other developers as people just because we're personally frustrated with them.

The solution isn't just to say "everybody, now bottle up your frustrations until you explode," though. There are lots of practical solutions. One of the best is to set up some specific system for handling problematic contributors. If there's some contributor that Bob just can't live with, there needs to be somebody in the community who Bob can go to help work things out.

We'll call this go-to person the "community moderator." So Bob tells the moderator about the problem, and maybe the moderator sees that other contributor really was being a terrible person or bad coder, and so this "community moderator" gently corrects that contributor. But it's also possible that there was some communication problem between Bob and the other contributor that the moderator just needs to help resolve.

This "moderator" system isn't the only way to deal with the problem. You can resolve the problem in numerous ways – the most important thing is that you *do* resolve it. Without some channel or method for dealing with personal frustrations, individual contributors will take these frustrations out on each other. You will in fact foster an environment where it's *okay* for one contributor to personally attack another contributor, because that's the only avenue they have to resolve their problems, and nobody's stopping them.

Basically, those last two points can be summed up as: **be really, abnormally, really, really kind, and don't be mean**.

We applied all of these principles in the Bugzilla Project for the past several months, and we saw an increase in the number of retained contributors almost immediately after we started applying them. It finally started to feel like the community was *growing* again, after shrinking almost continuously from 2005 to 2010 due to violations of all of the above points.

Removing the Barriers

The next step is to remove the *barriers to entry*. What prevents people from getting started on the project?

Usually, the biggest barrier is a lack of documentation and direction. When people already *want* to contribute, their next step is figuring out *how* to contribute. They will go to your project's website and look around. They will wonder, "Who do I talk to about this? How do I start contributing? What do you guys want me to work on?"

For the Bugzilla Project, we solved this problem in several ways:

1. A list of easy starting projects

Whenever we see a bug or feature request that looks like it would be easy for a newcomer to solve, we tag it as a "good intro bug" in our bug tracker. This gives us a list of good introductory projects that anybody can come and look at without having to ask us "where do I get started?"

2. Create and document communication channels

People will almost immediately want to *talk* to somebody else about the project. You should have email lists and also some method of instantaneous communication like an IRC channel. For example, we have an email list for Bugzilla developers and also an IRC channel where almost all our contributors hang out.

In fact, we don't just have a normal IRC channel – we also have a web page that people can use to chat in that IRC channel. That way, people don't have to install an IRC client just to come talk to us. Setting up that web page enormously increased the number of new people coming into the channel and communicating with us. (And the increase was entirely positive – I can't think of a single person who used the web gateway to cause us trouble.)

Then once you have these channels, they need to be documented! People have to know how to get into them, they need to know that they exist. We have a wiki page that explains how to talk to us if you want to contribute:

```
https://wiki.mozilla.org/Bugzilla:Communicate
```

that explains how to talk to us if you want to contribute. (Note that this is separate from our support page that describes how to get support for the project.)

Also, as a final but perhaps obvious point, the existing community has to *use* the communication channels. If the main contributors do all their work in an office and just talk to the people next to then and you don't use the mailing lists or IRC channels, then the community members aren't going to want to use those communication systems either. After all, the new contributors aren't there to talk to each other – they're there to talk to *you*!

3. Excellent, complete, and simple documentation, describing exactly how a contribution should be done

Fully document every step of your development process, and put that documentation onto a public web site. Don't invent a new process, just document out what the existing actual process is. How do people get the code? How can they submit patches or other contributions to you? How do those contributions become an official part of the system?

We have a very simple page that describes the basic steps of our whole process, and links to documents that describe each step in more detail:

```
https://wiki.mozilla.org/Bugzilla:Developers
```

The page also specifically encourages people to get into communication with us, so that we know that they are there and want to help.

4. Make all this documentation easy to find

This is a simple final step, but sometimes projects forget it! You can have all the wonderful developer documentation in the world, but if new contributors can't find it *super-easily*, then you're not actually removing any barriers to entry! We have a big "Contribute!" button on the homepage of bugzilla.org that describes all the different ways that people can contribute (not just code!) and links to more information about each of those.

We saw a definite upswing in the number and quality of contributions once we completed all these steps. Also, having everything documented and clearly stated on a public website meant that we no longer had to personally explain it all, every time, to every new contributor.

Direction and documentation aren't the *only* things you can do though. Ask yourself, "What is stopping people from contributing?" and remove all the barriers there that you reasonably can.

Getting People Interested

How do you make people think, "Gee, I want to contribute to this project?" That's the first step they have to take before they can become contributors. Well, traditional wisdom states that people contribute to open-source projects because:

♦ They like helping

♦ They enjoy being part of a community

♦ They want to give back

♦ They think that something is wrong and they need/ want to fix it

So you may want to make it apparent that help is needed, that an enjoyable community is there, that giving back is appropriate and appreciated, and that there are problems that need solving.

Now, to be fair, this is an area that I don't have fully mapped out or figured out for the Bugzilla Project, yet. So I don't have a lot of personal experience to draw on. But if we analyze other projects, we can see that some good ways of getting contributors...

Be a super-popular product

This may seem obvious, but it is indeed the primary way of getting new contributors. If a zillion people use your product, it's statistically likely that many of them will want to contribute. The Linux Kernel and WordPress are good examples of this – they have millions of users, so there's just bound to be a lot of contributors, provided that the "barriers to entry" and the "retaining contributors" aspects of the project have also been handled.

One way to *become* a super-popular product – even if you're just starting out – is to be *heavily needed*. The Linux Kernel was very much needed when it was first written, which is probably one of the reasons that it became popular as quickly as it did. It desperately needed to exist and didn't exist yet.

Be written in a popular programming language

Generally, people are more likely to contribute to a project if it's written in a language that they already know. WordPress has a *huge* contributor community, and it's in PHP. Say what you will about PHP, it is extremely popular. There's a large number of people who already know the language, which increases the likelihood that some of them will start supplying patches for your code.

This not the only reason you should choose a particular programming language, but it's certainly a major motivator if you're going to have an open-source project. I may think that Eiffel (https://www.eiffel.org/) is a remarkable language, but if I wrote an open-source project in it, I would have a *very* hard time getting contributors.

Beyond those points, there are lots of clever ways of getting people interested in contributing to your projects, including speaking at conferences, publishing blogs, encouraging people on a one-to-one basis, and other methods that basically add up to "contact and encourage."

I'd love to hear some of your ideas in this area, though. How do you get new people interested in contributing to your project? Has anything been particularly successful?

Summary

An open-source community is somewhat of a fluid thing — there are always going to be people coming and going for one reason or another. What's important is that the rate of people entering and staying is *greater* than the rate of people leaving. All of these points help assure that, and hopefully they also make our communities productive and enjoyable places to be for everybody, even ourselves!

-Max

PART SIX

UNDERSTANDING
SOFTWARE

~ 24 ~

WHAT IS A COMPUTER?

In order to understand software, the first thing we need to understand is what a computer *really is*.

Now, you'd think that would be a fairly simple question. After all, I'm using one to type this up, I ought to know what it is, right? I mean obviously, it's a...computer! I mean, it's got a keyboard, and a monitor, and there's that box down there...

But what is it that makes all that stuff a *computer*? Why do we look at it and go, "Oh yeah, that's a computer," as opposed to, say, "Oh, that's just a TV," or "That's where I keep the leprechauns at night."?

Some people try to define the word "computer" just by saying "it's got such and such parts and they all work this way," but that's like saying "airplanes have two wings and jet engines." It's true, but I could build an airplane that *didn't* have two wings or jet engines. The way something *works* is not a *definition* for that thing.

Others try to define it mathematically, but that can also be somewhat limiting, because then only the devices that fit into your mathematical scheme are computers, and there are multiple mathematical models that could be considered "computers."

So I turned to the dictionary. That was fun for me – I'm a dictionary fanatic. I've got lots of great dictionaries, and there are even more online. The *Compact Oxford English Dictionary* had a definition that was almost good enough:

computer

noun

> an electronic device capable of storing and processing information in accordance with a predetermined set of instructions.

I was very happy with the definition at first, but when I started to think about it, it didn't quite work. For example, it calls computers "an electronic device," but computers could be built without electronics. After all, Charles Babbage designed the first device we might consider a computer in the 1800s, and it wasn't electronic at all.

So I worked to come up with a definition of my own. Strangely enough, the key question that it boiled down to was "Why is a player piano *not* a computer?" It "processes information" by playing notes from its roll. If you gave it an etching machine, it could "store information" back on to the roll. But despite all that, it's clearly not a computer. What is a computer doing that is fundamentally different from a player piano, that a player piano could *never* do?

After about two years, I finally came up with an answer that was both simple and all-encompassing:

> **A computer is any piece of matter which can carry out a series of symbolic instructions and compare data in assistance of a human goal.**

And that, my friends, is really it. Note several important things about this definition:

♦ A computer can compare data. This is what separates a computer from other machines that take input from people.

♦ The computer doesn't just take one instruction, but a series of them. A simple calculator can only carry out one instruction, which is what differentiates it from a computer.

♦ A mouse click is a "symbolic instruction," as is pressing a key on a keyboard. However, as programmers, the primary symbolic instructions we use in our craft are programming languages. Thus we as programmers, when we talk about how to improve the quality of our work, care mostly about how our programs are structured.

This is perhaps an obvious statement, but it provides the logical basis for why I'm about to talk so much about the philosophy behind how software is organized, in the next few chapters.

-Max

∾ 25 ∾

THE
COMPONENTS
OF SOFTWARE:
STRUCTURE,
ACTION, AND
RESULTS

There's a very popular model for designing software that we've all heard of if we're web developers, and probably most desktop developers have heard of too: our old friend Model-View-Controller.

This works well because it reflects the basic nature of a computer program: a series of *actions* taken on a *structure* of data to produce a *result*. Programs also take input, and so you could possibly argue that input was a fourth part of a program, but usually I just think of a computer program as the first three parts: Structure, Action, and Results.

In the MVC sense, the Model is the Structure, the Controller is what does the Actions, and the View is the Result. I think the analogy (and the words) Structure, Action, and Results are more widely and accurately applicable to the operation of every program in existence, though, more so than MVC, although MVC is a perfectly good way of looking at it for GUI applications.

> **Structure, Action, and Results probably describes almost any machine in existence.**

A machine has some parts that don't move, a framework — that's the structure. Some parts move and do something — that motion is the action. And of course the machine produces something (otherwise we wouldn't care much about it) so that's the result.

Computer programs are unusual machines in that they can modify their own structure. However, it's important that some part of the program be stable, that they "not move" in a logical sense. The way that object classes relate to each other, the names of methods and variables — these are all parts of the structure that usually don't change while you're running.

Of course, sometimes you make new classes, methods, or variables while you're running, but they usually follow some pre-set plan, so there's still a lot of "not moving" involved.

> **When I'm writing software, I usually build the Structure first, then I work on the Actions, and then I work on the displaying of the Result.**

Some people work backwards from the Results, that's fine too. Probably the only inadvisable thing to do is to start with the Actions, since it's kind of confusing to be performing Actions without a Structure and with no defined Result.

There's so much to this concept that I could probably write a whole book just on this one topic, but I think this is a decent introduction, and I'm sure that given this, you can think of lots of other useful applications of it.

-Max

～26～

SOFTWARE REVISITED: (I)SAR CLARIFIED

In the last chapter, I said that there are three major parts to any computer program: *Structure*, *Action*, and *Results*.

Now also, a program has *Input*, which could be considered a fourth part of the program, although usually it's not the programmer who's creating the input, but the user. So we can either abbreviate this as SAR or ISAR, depending on whether or not we want to include "Input."

Now, some people misunderstood me and said, "Oh, SAR is just another name for MVC." No, I used MVC as an example of SAR, but SAR is a much, much broader concept than MVC – they are not comparable theories.

> **MVC is a pattern for designing software, whereas SAR (or ISAR) is a statement of the three (or four) components that are present in *all software*.**

The fascinating thing about SAR is that it applies not only to a whole program, but also to any *piece* of that program. A whole program has a Structure, just as a function or single line of code has a Structure. Same for Action and Results.

Here's a little more about each of these pieces, and some examples to help explain.

Structure

Here are some examples of things that would be considered "Structure" for the whole program:

♦ The directory layout of your code.

♦ All of the classes and how they relate to each other.

♦ The structure (schema) of the database, if your program uses a database.

Note here that the actual data in the database isn't part of the Structure, though. If your program is *producing* the data and then sticking it into the database, then that's part of the *Result*. If the data is sitting in the database and your program is supposed to process it, then that data is part of the *Input*.

Then an individual class (and I mean a "class" in the object-oriented sense) would also have a Structure:

♦ The names of methods in the class and the types/ names of parameters that they take.

♦ The names and types of variables (member variables) in the class.

Whether or not a function (or variable) is private or public would also be part of the Structure, because Structure describes what something *is* (as opposed to what it *does* or *produces*), and "private" or "public" are words that describe what something *is*.

A Structure is sort of "the components of the program" or "the pieces you make the program out of." Function names and types, variable names and types, classes — these things are all *Structure*.

Structure just "sits there." It doesn't *do* anything unless there's some part of your program that *uses* it. For example, a method doesn't call *itself*, it just sits there waiting to be called. A variable doesn't put data into itself, it just sits there waiting for you to do something with it.

Action

The *Action* of a whole program is very easy to understand. A tax program "does taxes." A calculator program "does math."

An Action is always a *verb* of some sort. "Calculates." "Fixes." "Adds." "Removes." Those are *actions*. Usually they're a little more descriptive and specific, though, like, "Calculates how much rainfall there will be in Africa next year," or "Fixes broken hard drives."

Inside of a class, the *Action* is the code *inside* of the methods. That's all some sort of *action* — something going on, something happening. In many programming languages, you can also have code outside of any class or function — code that just runs when you start the program. That's *Action*.

Results

Every program, every function, and every line of code has some *effect*. It produces some *result*.

A Result can always be talked about in the *past tense* – it's something that *has been* done or created. "Calculated rainfall," or "Fixed hard drives." In a tax program, we'd call the Result either *filed taxes* or *filled-out tax forms*. As you can see, it sounds a lot like the Action, just *completed*.

You don't *have* to describe a Result in the past tense, though. I'm just saying it always *can be* described that way. For example, in a calculator program, normally we'd call the Result of addition "the sum," (not past-tense, just a noun) but you could also say that the Result is "added numbers" (which is past-tense). Same thing, just a different way of describing it.

Individual pieces of your program have Results, too. When you call a method or function, it has a very specific Result. It gives you back some data, or it causes some data to be changed.

Whatever your program (or any part of your program) *produces*, that's the Result.

ISAR in a Single Line of Code

So, I said that SAR applies to a single line of code, but I didn't give you any examples. So here's a single line of code:

```
x = y + z
```

y and z in that line are part of the Structure. They're variables that hold some data. To make an analogy: A jug is a structure that holds water. A variable is a structure that holds data.

The numbers that are stored inside y and z are the *Input*. That's the data that we're doing something with.

+ is an Action: "Add these two numbers."

= is also an Action: "Store the result in x."

And, of course, the Result is the sum of y and z that gets stored in x. If y is 1 and z is 2, then the Result is the number 3, which gets stored in x. (Also note that x is itself a variable and thus also part of the Structure, but that's getting pretty technical.)

Wrapping SAR Up

SAR is a concept that applies to any kind of programming, whether you're building a big application or just writing a single-line script. It's not something that you have to think about in-depth every time you write a piece of code, but it can help us analyze and understand a program – particularly when we're looking at how we can improve its design.

-Max

~ 27 ~

SOFTWARE AS KNOWLEDGE

I don't often dive deep into the philosophical underpinnings of my writings, but I've been realizing more and more that there are a few philosophical principles behind my ideas that it would be valuable to share. So that's what this chapter is about.

Also, some of these philosophies weren't fully formed until I sat with the work for a long time, applied it in a lot of situations, and talked about it with many people. This particular idea — a theory that I have developed over time about how software can be thought of and worked with in the mind — has sort of been percolating with me for quite a while now. It's time to get at least part of it out on paper. So here you go.

> **Software is, fundamentally, a solid object that is made of knowledge. It follows all the rules and laws of knowledge. It behaves exactly as knowledge behaves in just about any given situation, except that it's in concrete form.**

For example, when software is complex it tends to be misused. When software is wrong (i.e., has a bug), it tends to cause harm or problems. When people don't understand some code, they tend to alter it incorrectly. One could say these things of knowledge just as one could say them of software. Bad data causes people to misbehave; bad code causes computers to misbehave. I'm not saying that computers and people can be compared — I'm saying that software and knowledge can be.

One wishes to have knowledge in a sensible and logical form. Similarly, one should also desire to have software — particularly the code — in a sensible and logical form. Because code *is* knowledge, it should translate to knowledge in one's mind almost immediately upon viewing it. If it doesn't, then some part of it is too complex — perhaps the underlying programming language or systems, but more likely the structure of the code as created by its designer.

When we desire knowledge, there are numerous ways to acquire it. One could read about it, think about it, perform observations, do experiments, talk about it, etc. In general, we could divide these methods into acquiring the data for ourselves (via observation, experiment, thought, etc.) or getting data from somebody else (reading, talking, etc.).

There are some situations in which we *must* get data for ourselves, particularly when it applies to us in some unique way that we couldn't rely on others to work out correctly. As an extreme example, walking on my own legs likely took tremendous amounts of personal experimentation when my body was much smaller. I probably had some assistance, but that knowledge *had* to be developed by me.

There are far more situations, however, in which we must rely on secondhand data. If one wants to do a good job at living, there's a lot to know — one simply could not acquire so much information on their own. This is where the help of others comes in: the data they know, the lessons they've learned and can teach us.

It seems likely that these same principles describe when one should write code themselves or use existing code. You pretty much *couldn't* write all the code yourself down to the hardware level and come up with some of the most useful software we have today.

For sure, there are some things that only we are uniquely qualified to write — usually the specific logic of the product that we're working on. But there are many more things that we must rely on existing code for, just like we must rely on existing secondhand knowledge to survive as individuals.

It's also possible we could use this principle somewhat for deciding how to divide up work between developers. Would it be faster for somebody to create a piece of code out of their firsthand knowledge, or would it be faster for a group of people to look at the existing system (secondhand knowledge) and start to contribute their own parts (which will, in time, essentially become their firsthand knowledge)?

The answer depends on the situation, obviously, and though the basic idea here may not be too novel (some programmers already know the system better than others and so they're faster) the way we *came* to the idea is what matters. We first theorize that software is knowledge, and then suddenly we can see a clear logical line down to some existing principle that is already known to be generally true. Pretty handy, and indicates we could likely derive other, more useful information from this principle.

Of course, this is not, by itself, a science or a scientific system. It's just an idea, one that seems to work well for deriving principles about development. I would say it is one of the broadest philosophical theories that I've been able to develop about software, in fact.

It seems to cover all aspects and explain all behaviors. I could actually sit here and theorize about this idea for a long time, but my goal in this chapter is to give you a brief summary and then let you explore what you see when you look into the matter of software: knowledge.

-Max

~ 28 ~

THE PURPOSE OF
TECHNOLOGY

In general:

> **When technology attempts to solve
> problems of matter, energy, space, or
> time, it is successful. When it attempts
> to solve human problems of the mind,
> communication, ability, etc. it fails or
> backfires dangerously.**

For example, the Internet handled a great problem of space
– it allowed us to communicate with anybody in the world,
instantly. However, it did not make us better communicators.
In fact, it took many poor communicators and gave them a
massive platform on which they could spread hatred and fear.

This isn't me saying that the Internet is all bad – I'm actually quite fond of it, personally. I'm just giving an example to demonstrate what types of problems technology does and does not solve successfully.

> **The reason this principle, or rule, is useful is that it tells us in advance what kind of software purposes or startup ideas are more likely to be successful.**

Companies that focus on solving human problems with technology are likely to fail. Companies that focus on resolving problems that can be expressed in terms of material things at least have the *possibility* of success.

Are there Counter-Examples to this Rule?

There can be some seeming counter-examples to this rule. For example, isn't the purpose of Facebook to connect people? That sounds like a human problem, and Facebook is very successful. But connecting people is not actually what Facebook does. It provides a medium through which people can communicate, but it doesn't actually create or cause human connection. In fact, most people I know seem to have a sort of uncomfortable feeling of addiction surrounding Facebook – the sense that they are spending more time there than is valuable for them as people.

So I'd say that Facebook is exacerbating certain human problems (like a craving for connection) wherever it focuses on solving those problems. But it's achieving other purposes (removing space and time from broad communication) excellently.

Once again, this isn't an attack on Facebook, which I think is a well-intentioned company; it's an attempt to make an objective analysis of what aspects of its purpose are successful using the principle that technology only solves physical problems.

Is the Advance of Technology "Good"?

This rule is also useful in clarifying whether or not the advance of technology is "good." I've had mixed feelings at times about the advance of technology — was it really giving us a better world, or was it making us all slaves to machines? The answer is that technology is neither inherently good nor bad, but it does *tend* towards evil when it attempts to solve human problems, and it does tend toward good when it focuses on solving problems of the material universe.

Ultimately, our current civilization could not exist without technology, which includes things like public sanitation systems, central heating, running water, electrical grids, and the very computer that I am writing this essay on. Technology is in fact a vital force that is necessary to our existence, but we should remember that it is not the answer to *everything* — it's not going to make us better people. But it can make us live in a better world.

-Max

~ 29 ~

PRIVACY, SIMPLIFIED

So, there's a lot of talk on the Internet about privacy. Some people say that privacy is only desired by those who have something to hide. Some people insist that privacy is a human right that should never be violated without consent.

There's only one problem with this whole debate: what is privacy, and why would anybody want it? This is rarely defined — most people just seem to assume that "everybody knows" what privacy is, so why would it have to be explained?

Well, I'm not a big fan of "everybody knows." And in fact, it turns out that privacy actually means two different things, which many people use interchangeably without specifying what they're actually talking about. So to help clear up some of the debate online, and to hopefully shed some light on how it can all be resolved, here are some clear definitions and discussions of what privacy is, and why people would want it.

Privacy of Space

The first type of privacy is "privacy of space". This is the ability to control who does and does not enter a particular physical space, probably because you're in the space and you don't want certain others in that space. "Enter the space" in that definition includes any method of being able to perceive the space — so, for example, if somebody stands outside the door with their ear pressed to it, they're violating your privacy. If somebody installs a camera in your room without your consent, they're violating your privacy.

This form of privacy is not metaphorical. It does not apply to anything other than physical space. It literally means, "I do or do not want you to be perceiving this physical location, and I have the choice and ability to control that."

The most common reason that we want this form of privacy is that we want to protect somebody or something from harm, most commonly ourselves. This harm can be minor (we don't want to be annoyed by people walking through our house all the time), it can be purely social (we close the door when we go to the bathroom because we know others don't want to perceive us going to the bathroom, and we may also not want to be perceived in such a state), or it can be extreme (a man with a mask and a chainsaw should not be in my closet).

One interesting thing about this form of privacy is that we don't usually consider animals, plants, or material objects to be capable of violating it, even if they enter a space without our permission. It might be *annoying* if the cat comes in the room when you don't want it to, but you're not going to complain that the cat is "violating your privacy", right?

> **So, when it comes to computer programs, this is *not* the form of privacy we're talking about, since we don't consider that a computer program being in the same room with us is a violation of our privacy of space.**

My word processor is not violating my physical privacy of space, even though it's "in the room" with me, because it does not, itself, perceive. The only exception would be a computer program that was transmitting perceptions (sound or sight) to some location that we didn't want to send it to – that would be a privacy violation, because someone could perceive our space through it when we didn't want them to.

When it comes to that sort of privacy, violations are pretty cut-and-dry. If a computer program sends perceptions of my space anywhere without my permission, it is absolutely violating my privacy, it's not useful to me, and it should stop immediately. But on the Internet, that's not usually the type of privacy we're talking about.

Privacy of Information

The second type of privacy is "privacy of information." This is the ability to control who *knows* certain things. When we talk about computer programs and the Internet, *this* is the most common type of privacy we're talking about.

So why would somebody want privacy of information? Is it just because they're doing something that they want to hide from others? Is it just for committing crimes or for hiding harmful acts? Well, sometimes it is, yes. There are many people who use the concept of "privacy" to protect themselves from the law or the moral rejection of others. It is probably because of these individuals that the concept of privacy is a muddy subject — as long as it's unclear quite what "privacy" is, it's much easier for those who have committed harmful acts to invoke "privacy" as a defense.

But is that the *only* reason that somebody would want privacy of information? What about a normal person, who isn't doing anything harmful — would they ever want to keep certain information private?

Well, there is absolutely a rational reason that people would want privacy of information, and interestingly, it's the same reason that people want privacy of space:

> **An individual or group desires privacy of information because they believe that other people knowing that information could or would be more harmful than them not knowing it.**

Here's a very straightforward example: I consider that a criminal knowing my credit card number would be harmful — far more harmful than them not knowing it.

In certain countries, the fact that I read a certain website or talked to certain people on the Internet could get me killed or put in jail. So, in that situation, other people knowing my browser history could be very harmful, no question about it.

Of course, if one kept everything private, one could not live. If you pay for a piece of candy with a quarter, the person receiving that quarter now knows that you had a quarter. They may know that you kept it in a wallet, or that you pulled it out of your pants. They probably know what you look like, if you're not wearing a mask. They most likely also know that you have five fingers, and that you were in their store at a certain time.

> **In short, no matter what you do, in order to live, you must exchange information with other people. The more things you do, the more information you will have to exchange.**

In fact, usually, the more information that others know about you, the more helpful they can be. The bank knows all the transactions that I made, so they can help me by creating an online system that shows me my transactions and lets me search them. That information can be seen by bank employees, but I don't consider that to be potentially harmful *enough* to outweigh the obvious benefits of the bank having it.

The web browsers that I use know my passwords to certain sites, so they can help me by putting those passwords into the box, saving me some typing. Potentially, somebody could steal that information from my computer, but the chance of that happening is small enough, and the benefit is significant enough, so I consider it acceptable to save my passwords in the browser.

The examples like this go on and on – the appropriate use of information is extremely beneficial. The *inappropriate* use is what's harmful.

So who decides what what's an appropriate use and what's an inappropriate use? What information should be sent and stored, and what information should be kept private? Well, these are the fundamental questions being asked when people debate privacy issues – who gets to choose whether my knowledge becomes somebody else's knowledge? Should I be asked before my information is sent, or should I just be given the option to opt-out and delete the information? Is there some information that should never be sent? What information is more important to keep private than other information?

Though this is all far less cut-and-dry than "privacy of space" issues, these questions can generally be answered by the "help vs harm" equation.

The basic sort of questions one might want to ask would be:

♦ Will sending and storing this information harm *any* users, immediately or potentially? (Remember, "potentially" is pretty broad – what happens if somebody with bad intentions steals that information from you? What happens if somebody buys your company and decides to use that information in a way that you think is bad?)

- Would it help your users more than harm them to take this information?

- Taking all the above into account, should sending this information be optional? (This is largely determined by how broadly it *could* be harmful to collect the information.)

- If sending the information is optional, should it be opt-out or opt-in? (That is, should it automatically be on, and people have to turn it off if they don't want to send the info, or should it be off and people have to choose to turn it on?)

- If it's opt-in, will the feature still be helpful to enough of your users to justify implementing it?

There are some people who will claim that no information should ever be sent or stored about the user, that all privacy options should always be opt-in, and that all information is so potentially harmful that no debate about this can be accepted. That is, frankly, a ridiculous proposition. It's so obviously untrue that there's almost no way to argue with it, because it's such a shocking irrationality. Just like the fact that somehow, liquids could harm somebody (so you can't bring liquids on an airplane in the USA). It's true that there are situations in which almost any piece of information *could* be dangerous. That doesn't mean that all information is dangerous, though.

My martial artist friends have frequently joked that they shouldn't be allowed to bring *any* object on an airplane, because they could kill somebody with any of them. Similarly, given almost *any* piece of information, somebody could do *something* harmful with it, somewhere, at some point. If I know you have a quarter in your pocket, I'm sure there's some situation in which I could use that information to get you in some serious trouble. But that doesn't make that information realistically harmful, even potentially.

Even the idea of "every single piece of information should be opt-in" is ridiculous. Do you want the web browser to ask you, "May I send this page your IP address?" every time you load a web page? Well, if you're a spy in a hostile country, maybe you do. But if you're like most people, that would probably just annoy you – you'd stop using that web browser and switch to another one. And if you *are* a spy or a resistance fighter, then you probably know how to use Tor to avoid being tracked.

A Summary of Privacy

So when we're talking about privacy, it's really not an issue of "in some incredibly unlikely situation, this information could be very harmful," it's an issue of balancing help versus harm in real-world situations.

Real-world situations can be pretty strange and unexpected, but they at least are *real*, and can be balanced and talked about. Doing so, you can make good decisions about how to protect your users' privacy – how much information to take, how you inform them about the information you're taking, and what you do with that information when you have it.

So no, this is not a casual issue or something that we should just brush-off, ignoring the dangerous implications that come with it. And yet neither is this an extreme or unsolvable situation, where we have to decide to keep everything private, just because we can't make up our minds about it.

Privacy is simply something that we should be able to analyze factually, based on real-world situations and data, and come to some practical and useful decision about.

-Max

~ 30 ~

SIMPLICITY AND SECURITY

A big part of writing secure software (probably the biggest part) is simplicity.

When we think about software security, the first question that we ask is, "How many different ways could this program possibly be attacked?" That is, how many "ways in" are there? It's a bit like asking "How many doors and windows are there on this building?" If your building has 1 exterior door, it's very easy to protect that door. If it has 1000, it will be impossible to keep the building secure, no matter how good the doors are or how many security guards you have.

So we need to limit the "ways in" to our software to some reasonable number, or it won't ever be secure. That's accomplished by making the *overall system* relatively simple, or breaking it down into very simple and totally separate component parts.

Then, once we've limited the ways in, we need to start thinking about:

"How many different possible attacks are there against each way in?"

We limit that by making the "ways in" *themselves* very simple. Like a door with only one unique key, instead of a door that can take five different keys, all of which individually will open the door.

Once that's done, we limit how much damage any attack could do if it got through. For example, in a building, we'd make any given door only allow access to one room.

All of this explains, for example, why earlier versions of Windows were fundamentally flawed and would *never* be secure, and why UNIX-based systems have a better reputation for security.

Standard UNIX has a very small number of system calls that are used to implement the vast majority of all UNIX programs out there. (Even the extended list is only about 140 system calls, though most of those are never used by the average program.) Each system call is extremely specific and does one very limited thing.

Windows, on the other hand, has a ridiculous set of system calls that are confusing, take too many arguments, and do too much.

Going up to a higher level in the system, the Windows API is massive and complex. It's a strange beast that controls both the OS and the GUI. There's really no equivalent thing in UNIX (because the OS and the GUI are separate), but we can at least compare parts of it. For instance if we compare the Windows Logging API and the Linux Logging API, there's no comparison at all – it's like a joke. There are so many "ways in" to any part of Windows that it will never be fundamentally secure.

You might say, "Well, I haven't had a virus on my Windows machine in a long time." That's not what I'm talking about – I'm talking about *fundamental* security. In order to have a secure Windows machine, you have to have a firewall that asks you every time a program wants to make an outbound connection. You have to have a spyware scanner. You have to have antivirus software that slows down your computer by as much as 2000%. If Windows was secure, you wouldn't need those things.

When we design our own systems, keeping them simple is the only real guarantee of security. We keep each "way in" to the system as simple as possible, and we never add more "ways in" than we absolutely need. These are compatible things, too, because the simpler each "way in" is, the *fewer* we'll actually need. That may not make sense until you think about it this way: If all actions on the system can be reduced to, say, 13 fundamental function calls, then the user can do *everything* with those 13 calls, even if they're not very powerful individually. If instead we only let them do 100 different specific tasks, and *don't* allow them to use the 13 fundamental calls, we have to add a new function for *every specific task*.

There are lots of other "ways in" to a program than just its public API, too. How the user interface interacts with the backend — that involves various "ways in". Can we access this program's internal structure from another program? That would be another "way in." There are *lots* of ways to apply this principle. Any way you slice it, though:

> ## The best way to get real security in things is *simplicity*.

We shouldn't have to put a small army in front of our software just to keep it secure. It should just fundamentally have so few "ways in" that it doesn't need the protection, and those "ways in" should be so streamlined and simple that they're impossible to exploit.

-Max

∽ 31 ∽

TEST-DRIVEN DEVELOPMENT AND THE CYCLE OF OBSERVATION

I recently watched an interesting discussion between several well-known programmers on the nature and use of TDD (Test-Driven Development), a development system where one writes tests first and then writes code.

Each participant in the conversation had different personal preferences for how they write code, which makes sense. However, from each participant's personal preference you could extract an identical principle: "I need to observe something before I can make a decision." Some wanted to observe the results of the tests while they were writing code, while others wanted to write code and look at *that* to decide how to write further code. Even when they talked about exceptions to their own rules, they always talked about *having something to look at* as a fundamental part of their development process.

It's possible to minimize this point and say it's only relevant to debugging or testing. It's true that it's useful in those areas, but when you talk to many senior developers you find that this idea is actually a fundamental basis of their whole development workflow. They want to see *something* that will help them make decisions about their code. It's not something that only happens when code is complete or when there's a bug – it's something that happens at every moment of the software lifecycle.

This is such a broad principle that you could say the cycle of all software development is:

> **Observation → Decision → Action → Observation → Decision → Action → etc.**

If you want a term for this, you could call it the "Cycle of Observation" or "ODA."

Examples of ODA

What do I mean by all of this? Well, let's take some examples to make it clearer. When doing TDD, the cycle looks like this:

1. See a problem (observation).

2. Decide to solve the problem (decision).

3. Write a test (action).

4. Look at the test and see if the API looks good (observation).

5. If it doesn't look good, decide how to fix it (decision), change the test (action), and repeat Observation → Decision → Action until you like what the API looks like.

6. Now that the API looks good, run the test and see that it fails (observation).

7. Decide how you're going to make the test pass (decision).

8. Write some code (action).

9. Run the test and see that it passes or fails (observation).

10. If it fails, decide how to fix it (decision) and write some code (action) until the test passes (observation).

11. Decide what to work on next, based on principles of software design, knowledge of the problem, or the data you gained while writing the previous code (decision).

12. And so on.

There are many valid processes of course. For example, another valid way to go here about this would be to write the code first. The difference from the above sequence is that Step 3 would be "write some code" rather than "write a test." Then you observe the code *itself* to make further decisions, or you write tests after the code and observe those.

Development Processes and Productivity

What's interesting is that, as far as I know, *every* valid development process follows this cycle as its primary guiding principle. Even large-scale processes like Agile that cover a whole team have this built into them. In fact, Agile is to some degree an attempt to have shorter Observation-Decision-Action cycles (every few weeks) for a team than previous broken models (Waterfall, aka "Big Design Up Front") which took months or years to get through a single cycle.

So, shorter cycles seem to be better than longer cycles. In fact, it's possible that most of the goal of developer productivity could be accomplished simply by shortening the ODA cycle down to the smallest reasonable time period for the developer, the team, or the organization.

Usually you can accomplish these shorter cycles just by focusing on the Observation step. Once you've done that, the other two parts of the cycle tend to speed up on their own. (If they don't, there are other remedies, but that's another story.)

There are three key factors to address in Observation:

♦ The **speed** with which information can be delivered to developers. (For example, having fast tests.)

♦ The **completeness** of information delivered to the developers. (For example, having enough test coverage.)

♦ The **accuracy** of information delivered to developers. (For example, having reliable tests.)

This helps us understand the reasons behind the success of certain development tools in recent decades. Continuous Integration, production monitoring systems, profilers, debuggers, better error messages in compilers, IDEs that highlight bad code – almost everything that's "worked" has done so because it made Observation faster, more accurate, or more complete.

There is one catch – you have to deliver the information in such a way that it can actually be *received* by people. If you dump a huge sea of information on people without making it easy for them to find the specific data they care about, the data becomes useless. If nobody ever receives a production alert, then it doesn't matter.

If a developer is never sure of the accuracy of information received, then they may start to ignore it. You must successfully *communicate* the information, not just *generate* it.

The First ODA

There is a "big ODA cycle" that represents the whole process of software development – seeing a problem, deciding on a solution, and delivering it as software. Within that big cycle there are many smaller ones (see the need for a feature, decide on how the feature should work, and then write the feature). There are even smaller cycles within that (observe the requirements for a single change, decide on an implementation, write some code), and so on.

The trickiest part is the first ODA cycle in any of these sequences, because you have to make an observation with no previous decision or action.

For the "big" cycle, it may seem like you start off with nothing to observe. There's no code or computer output to see yet! But in reality, you start off with at least *yourself* to observe. You have your environment around you. You have other people to talk to, a world to explore. Your first observations are often not of code, but of something to solve in the real world that will help people somehow.

You can even view the process of Observation, itself, as its own little ODA cycle: look at the world, decide to put your attention on something, put your attention on that thing, observe it, decide based on that to observe something else, etc.

There are likely infinite ways to use this principle; I've just presented just a few examples here for you.

-Max

~ 32 ~

THE PHILOSOPHY OF TESTING

Much like we gain knowledge about the behavior of the physical universe via the scientific method, we gain knowledge about the behavior of our software via a system of assertion, observation, and experimentation called "testing."

There are many things one could desire to know about a software system. It seems that most often we want to know if it *actually* behaves like we intended it to behave. That is, we wrote some code with a particular intention in mind, does it actually do that when we run it?

> **In a sense, testing software is the reverse of the traditional scientific method, where you test the universe and then use the results of that experiment to refine your hypothesis.**

Instead, with software, if our "experiments" (tests) don't prove out our hypothesis (the assertions the test is making), we change the system we are testing.

That is, if a test fails, it hopefully means that our software needs to be changed, not that our test needs to be changed. Sometimes we do also need to change our tests in order to properly reflect the current state of our software, though.

It can seem like a frustrating and useless waste of time to do such test adjustment, but in reality it's a natural part of this two-way scientific method – sometimes we're learning that our tests are wrong, and sometimes our tests are telling us that our system is out of whack and needs to be repaired.

This can help us think about our testing – by examining the value, the assertions, the boundaries, the assumptions and the design of our tests. Let's look at these five aspects now.

Test Value

The purpose of a test is to deliver us knowledge about the system, and **knowledge has different levels of value**. For example, testing that 1 + 1 still equals two no matter what time of day it is doesn't give us valuable knowledge. However, knowing that my code still works despite possible breaking changes in APIs I depend on could be very useful, depending on the context. So in general:

> **One must know what knowledge one desires before one can create an effective and useful test.**

One must then judge the value of that information appropriately, to understand where to put time and effort into testing.

Test Assertions

Given that we want to *know* something in order for a test to be a test, **it must be asserting something** and then informing us about that assertion. Human testers can make qualitative assertions, such as whether or not a color is attractive. But automated tests must make assertions that computers can reliably make, which usually means asserting that some specific quantitative statement is true or false.

> **A test without an assertion is not a test.**

We are trying to *learn* something about the system by running the test: whether the assertion is true or false is the knowledge we are gaining.

Test Boundaries

Every test has certain **boundaries** as an inherent part of its definition. In much the same way that you couldn't design a single experiment to prove all the theories and laws of physics, it would be prohibitively difficult to design a single test that actually validated all the behaviors of any complex software system at once.

> **So when designing a test, you should know what it is actually testing, and what it is not testing.**

If it seems that you *have* made such a test, most likely you've combined many tests into one and those tests should be split apart.

Test Assumptions

Every test has a set of **assumptions** built into it, which it relies on in order to be effective within its boundaries. For example, if you are testing something that relies on access to a database, your test might make the assumption that the database is up and running (because some other test has already checked that that part of the code works).

If the database is *not* up and running, then the test neither passes nor fails — it instead provides you no knowledge at all. This tells us that:

> **All tests have at least three results – pass, fail, and unknown.**

Tests with an "unknown" result must *not* say that they failed — otherwise they are claiming to give us knowledge when in fact they are not.

Test Design

Because of the boundaries and assumptions that we've just been looking at, we need to design our suite of tests so that:

> **The full set of our tests, when combined, actually gives us all the knowledge we want to gain.**

Each individual test only gives us knowledge within its boundaries and assumptions; so how do we overlap those boundaries, so that they reliably inform us about the real behavior of the entire system? The answer to this question may also affect the design of the software system being tested, because some designs are harder to completely test than others.

The question of test design leads us into the many *methods* of testing being practiced today, so let's here examine **end to end testing**, **integration testing**, and **unit testing**.

End to End Testing

"End to end" testing is where you make an assertion that involves one complete "path" through the logic of the system. That is, you start up the whole system, perform some action at the entry point of user input, and check the result that the system produces. You don't care how things work internally to accomplish this goal, you just care about the input and result. That is generally true for all tests, but here we're testing at the outermost point of input into the system and checking the outermost result that it produces, only.

An example end to end test for creating a user account in a typical web application would be to start up a web server, a database, and a web browser, and use the web browser to actually load the account creation web page, fill it in, and submit it. Then you would assert that the resulting page somehow tells us the account was created successfully.

The idea behind end to end testing is that we gain fully accurate knowledge about our assertions because we are testing a system that is as close to "real" and "complete" as possible. All of its interactions and all of its complexity along the path we are testing are covered by the test.

The problem of using *only* end to end testing is that it makes it very difficult to actually get *all* of the knowledge about the system that we might desire. In any complex software system, the number of interacting components and the combinatorial explosion of paths through the code make it difficult or impossible to actually cover *all* the paths and make *all* the assertions we want to make.

It can also be difficult to maintain end to end tests, as small changes in the system's internals lead to many changes in the tests.

End to end tests are valuable, particularly as an initial stopgap for a system that entirely lacks tests. They are also good as sanity checks that your whole system behaves properly when put together. They have an important place in a test suite, but they are not, by themselves, a good long-term solution for gaining full knowledge of a complex system.

> **If a system is designed in such a way that it can *only* be tested via end-to-end tests, then that is a symptom of broad architectural problems in the code.**

These issues should be addressed through refactoring until one of the other testing methods can be used.

Integration Testing

This is where you take two or more full "components" of a system and specifically test how they behave when "put together." A component could be a code module, a library that your system depends on, a remote service that provides you data — essentially any part of the system that can be conceptually isolated from the rest of the system.

For example, in a web application where creating an account sends the new user an email, one might have a test that runs the account creation code (without going through a web page, just exercising the code directly) and checks that an email was sent. Or one might have a test that checks that account creation succeeds when one is using a real database – that "integrates" account creation and the database. Basically this is any test that is explicitly checking that two or more components behave properly when used together.

Compared to end to end testing, integration testing involves a bit more isolation of components as opposed to just running a test on the whole system as a "black box."

Integration testing doesn't suffer as badly from the combinatorial explosion of test paths that end to end testing faces, particularly when the components being tested are simple and thus their interactions are simple. If two components are *hard* to integration test due to the complexity of their interactions, this indicates that perhaps one or both of them should be refactored for simplicity.

Integration testing is also usually not a sufficient testing methodology on its own, as doing an analysis of an entire system purely through the *interactions* of components means that one must test a very large number of interactions in order to have a full picture of the system's behavior.

There is also a maintenance burden with integration testing similar to end to end testing, though not as bad – when one makes a small change in one component's behavior, one might have to then update the tests for all the other components that interact with it.

Unit Testing

This is where you take one component alone and test that it behaves properly. In our account creation example, we could have a series of unit tests for the account creation code, a separate series of unit tests for the email sending code, a separate series of unit tests for the web page where users fill in their account information, and so on.

Unit testing is most valuable when you have a component that presents strong guarantees to the world outside of itself and you want to validate those guarantees. For example, a function's documentation says that it will return the number "1" if passed the parameter "0." A unit test would pass this function the parameter "0" and assert that it returned the number "1." It would not check how the code *inside* of the component behaved – it would only check that the function's guarantees were met.

Usually, a unit test is testing one behavior of one function in one class/module. One creates a set of unit tests for a class/module that, when you run them all, cover all behavior that you want to verify in that module. However, this almost always means testing only the public API of the system; unit tests should be testing the *behavior* of the component, not its *implementation*.

Theoretically, if all components of the system fully define their behavior in documentation, then by testing that each component is living up to its documented behavior, you are in fact testing all possible behaviors of the entire system. When you change the behavior of one component, you only have to update a minimal set of tests around that component.

Obviously, unit testing works best when the system's components are reasonably separate and are simple enough that it's possible to fully define their behavior.

It is often true that if you cannot fully unit test a system, but instead *have* to do integration testing or end to end testing to verify behavior, some design change to the system is needed. (For example, components of the system may be too entangled and may need more isolation from each other.) Theoretically, if a system were well-isolated and had guarantees for all of the behavior of every function in the system, then no integration testing or end to end testing would be necessary. Reality is often a little different, though.

Reality

In reality, there is a scale of testing that has infinite stages between unit testing and end to end testing. Sometimes you're a bit between unit testing and integration testing. Sometimes your test falls somewhere between an integration test and an end to end test. Real systems usually require all sorts of tests along this scale in order to understand their behavior reliably.

For example, sometimes you're testing only one part of the system but its internals depend on other parts of the system, so you're implicitly testing those too. This doesn't make your test an Integration Test, it just makes it a unit test that is also testing other internal components implicitly – slightly larger than a unit test, and slightly smaller than an integration test. In fact, this is the sort of testing that is often the most effective.

Fakes

Some people believe that in order to do true "unit testing" you must write code in your tests that isolates the component you are testing from *every other component* in the system – even that component's internal dependencies. Some even believe that this "true unit testing" is the holy grail that all testing should aspire to. This approach is often misguided, for the following reasons.

1. An advantage of having tests for individual components is that when the system changes, you have to update fewer unit tests than you have to update with integration tests or end to end tests. If you make your tests more complex in order to isolate the component under test, that complexity could defeat this advantage, because you're adding more test code that has to be kept up to date anyway.

    For example, imagine you want to test an email sending module that takes an object representing a user of the system, and sends an email to that user. You could invent a "fake" user object – a completely separate class – just for your test, out of the belief that you should be "just testing the email sending code and not the user code." But then when the *real* User class changes its behavior, you have to update the behavior of the fake User class – and a developer might even forget to do this, making your email sending test now invalid because its assumptions (the behavior of the User object) are invalid.

2. The relationships between a component and its internal dependencies are often complex, and if you're not testing its real dependencies, you might not be testing its real behavior. This sometimes happens when developers fail to keep "fake" objects in sync with real objects, but it can also happen via failing to make a "fake" object as genuinely complex and full-featured as the "real" object.

   For example, in our email sending example above, what if real users could have seven different formats of username but the fake object only had one format, and this affected the way email sending worked? (Or worse, what if this didn't affect email sending behavior when the test was originally written, but it *did* affect email sending behavior a year later and nobody noticed that they had to update the test?) Sure, you could update the fake object to have equal complexity, but then you're adding even more of a maintenance burden for the fake object.

3. Having to add too many "fake" objects to a test indicates that there is a design problem with the system that should be addressed in the code of the system instead of being "worked around" in the tests.

   For example, it could be that components are too entangled — the rules of "what is allowed to depend on what" or "what are the layers of the system" might not be well-defined enough.

In general, it is not bad to have "overlap" between tests. That is, you have a test for the public APIs of the User code, and you have a test for the public APIs of the email sending code. The email sending code uses real User objects and thus also does a small bit of implicit "testing" on the User objects, but that overlap is okay. It's better to have overlap than to miss areas that you want to test.

Isolation via "fakes" *is* sometimes useful, though. One has to make a judgment call and be aware of the trade-offs above, attempting to mitigate them as much as possible via the design of your "fake" instances. In particular, fakes are worthwhile to add two properties to a test – **determinism** and **speed**.

Determinism

If nothing about the system or its environment changes, then the result of a test should not change. If a test is passing on my system today but failing tomorrow even though I haven't changed the system, then that test is unreliable. In fact, it is invalid as a test because its "failures" are not really failures – they're an "unknown" result disguised as knowledge. We say that such tests are "flaky" or "non-deterministic."

Some aspects of a system are genuinely non-deterministic. For example, you might generate a random string based on the time of day, and then show that string on a web page. In order to test this reliably, you would need two tests:

1. A test that uses the random-string generation code over and over to make sure that it properly generates random strings.

2. A test for the web page that uses a fake random-string generator that always returns the same string, so that the web page test is deterministic.

Of course, you would only need the fake in that second test if verifying the exact string in the web page was an important assertion. It's not that everything about a test needs to be deterministic – it's that the *assertions* it is making need to always be true or always be false if the system itself hasn't changed. If you weren't asserting anything about the string, the size of the web page, etc. then you would not need to make the string generation deterministic.

Speed

One of the most important uses of tests is that developers run them while they are editing code, to see if the new code they've written is actually working. As tests become slower, they become less and less useful for this purpose. Or developers continue to use them but start writing code more and more slowly because they keep having to wait for the tests to finish.

In general, a test suite should not take so long that a developer becomes distracted from their work and loses focus while they wait for it to complete. Existing research indicates this takes somewhere between 2 and 30 seconds for most developers. Thus, a test suite used by developers during code editing should take roughly that length of time to run. It might be okay for it to take a few minutes, but that wouldn't be ideal. It would definitely not be okay for it to take ten minutes, under most circumstances.

There are other reasons to have fast tests beyond just the developer's code editing cycle. At the extreme, slow tests can become completely useless if they only deliver their result after it is needed. For example, imagine a test that took so long, you only got the result after you had already released the product to users. Slow tests affect lots of processes in a software engineering organization – it's simplest for them just to be fast.

Sometimes there is some behavior that is inherently slow in a test. For example, reading a large file off of a disk. It can be okay to make a test "fake" out this slow behavior — for example, by having the large file in memory instead of on the disk. Like with all fakes, it is important to understand how this affects the validity of your test and how you will maintain this fake behavior properly over time.

It is sometimes also useful to have an extra suite of "slow" tests that *aren't* run by developers while they edit code, but are run by an automated system after code has been checked in to the version control system, or run by a developer right before they check in their code. That way you get the advantage of a fast test suite that developers can use while editing, but also the more-complete testing of real system behavior even if testing that behavior is slow.

Coverage

There are tools that run a test suite and then tell you which lines of system code actually got run by the tests. They say that this tells you the "test coverage" of the system. These can be useful tools, but it is important to remember that they don't tell you if those lines were actually tested, they only tell you that those lines of code were run. If there is no assertion about the behavior of that code, then it was never actually tested.

Conclusion – The Overall Goal of Testing

There are many ways to gain knowledge about a system, and testing is just one of them. We could also read its code, look at its documentation, talk to its developers, etc., and each of these would give us a *belief* about how the system behaves. However, testing **validates** our beliefs, and thus is particularly important out of all of these methods.

The overall goal of testing is then to gain valid knowledge about the system.

This goal overrides all other principles of testing – any testing method is valid as long as it produces that result.

However, some testing methods are more efficient than others: they can make it easier to create and maintain tests which produce *all* the information we desire. These methods should be understood and used appropriately – as your judgment dictates, and as they apply to the specific system you're testing.

-Max

—PART SEVEN—

SUCK LESS

~ 33 ~

THE SECRET
OF SUCCESS:
SUCK LESS

When I started working on Bugzilla (http://www.bugzilla.org) in 2004, it was a difficult time for the whole project. There were tremendous problems with the code, we hadn't gotten a major release out in two years, and a lot of the main developers had left to go do paid work.

But eventually, thanks to a bunch of new members in the Bugzilla community, we released Bugzilla 2.18. Hooray! Bells rang, birds sang, and there was much rejoicing.

However, in the space between Bugzilla 2.16 (which was before my time) and Bugzilla 2.18 (which was the first release that I helped get out), something very strange happened – we developed *serious competition*.

> **All of the sudden there were a bunch of new and competing bug-tracking systems, some of them open-source and some of them not, that people were actually *using*.**

At first it wasn't too worrisome. Bugzilla was pretty dominant in its field, and it's hard to lose that kind of position. But as time went on, there was more and more competition, and some people were predicting doom and gloom for Bugzilla. We were a tiny group of completely unpaid volunteers, and some of these competing products were being made by companies whose marketing and development resources absolutely *dwarfed* us.

And yet, with every release, our download numbers kept going up. And always significantly: 30-50% more than the previous release, every time.

And then we hit Bugzilla 3.0, and our download numbers nearly *doubled*. And they kept going up with every release from there, the whole time I was involved with the project. In 2009 we got over 10 times the number of downloads per release than we did in 2004. So how did we pull this off? Well, as far as I can tell:

> **All you have to do to succeed in software is to consistently suck less with every release.**

Nobody would say that Bugzilla 2.18 was *awesome*, but *everybody* would say that it *sucked less* than Bugzilla 2.16 did. Bugzilla 2.20 wasn't *perfect*, but without a doubt, it *sucked less* than Bugzilla 2.18. And then Bugzilla 3.0 fixed a *whole lot of sucking* in Bugzilla, and it got a *whole lot more downloads*.

Why is it that this worked?

Well, when people are deciding *at first* what software to use, they have varying criteria. Sometimes they just use what's presented to them by default on the computer. Sometimes they have a whole list of requirements and they do lots of research and pick the software that has all the features they need. But once they've picked a program, they will stick with it unless there is some compelling reason to leave. It's not like people constantly are looking for new software to replace yours – they only start looking when your software *just won't stop sucking.*

> **As long as you consistently suck less with every release, you will retain most of your users.**

You're fixing the things that bother them, so there's no reason for them to switch away. Even if you didn't fix *everything* in *this* release, if you *sucked less*, your users will have faith that *eventually*, the things that bother them will be fixed. New users will find your software, and they'll stick with it too. And in this way, your user count will increase steadily over time.

You have to get out releases frequently enough that people believe that you really *will* suck less, of course. If your new release never comes out, then effectively, your current release never stops sucking.

But what happens if you do release frequently, but instead of fixing the things in your software that suck, you just add new features that don't fix the sucking? Well, eventually the patience of the individual user is going to run out. They're not going to wait *forever* for your software to stop sucking.

I remember a particular piece of software that I used every day for years. It had a lot of great features and a nice user interface, but it would crash two or three times a week. I really liked the software in general, but man, the crashing *sucked*. I reported a bug about it, and the bug was ignored. I kept using it through *10 new releases*, and it still crashed. The upgrades brought lots of new features, but I didn't care about them. Remember, the feature set only mattered to me when I *first* picked the software. Now I just needed it to *suck less*.

But it never did.

So eventually, I went and looked for another piece of software that did the same thing, switched over, and I was happy with that one for a while.

But guess what? It had a bug that *really sucked*. It didn't happen very often, but when it did, boy was it a problem. But it sucked *less* than my old software, so I kept using it. Until one day, my patience ran out (after maybe 7 upgrades of the software), and I switched again.

Now I'm using a program that has half the feature set of either of the previous two programs. But, as a user, I'm the happiest I've ever been with this type of software. Because you know what? My new program sucks *hardly at all*. I mean, there are little things about it that suck, but supposedly a new release is coming out soon that will fix some of that sucking, and so I'm okay with it for now.

Would I have guessed this secret of success before I started working on Bugzilla? No. I would have told you the traditional wisdom — that a product succeeds or fails based on its feature set and user interface. But after 5 years on this project, managing our releases and watching our download count, I can tell you from my factual experience this strange thing:

> **All you have to do to succeed as a software project is to *suck less* with every release.**

It doesn't matter how much competition you have, or how many buzzword-friendly features you can cram into your interface. Just suck less, and you'll succeed.

-Max

∽ 34 ∽

HOW WE FIGURED OUT WHAT SUCKED

So, if you've just read the previous chapter, you may well be asking, "Okay, but how do you figure out what sucks?"

Well, some of it's really obvious. You press a button and the program takes 10 minutes to respond. That sucks pretty bad. You get 100 complaints a week about the UI of a particular page – okay, so that *sucks*.

Usually there are one or two HUGE things that really suck, and they're really obvious – those are the things to focus on first, even if they require a tremendous amount of work. For example, before Bugzilla 3.0, Bugzilla had to compile every single library and the entire script it was about to run, every time you loaded a page. This added several seconds to each page load, on slower machines, and at least 1 second on faster machines. So *performance* was one big obvious thing that sucked about Bugzilla. But even more importantly, the code of Bugzilla sucked. It was being read by *everybody* – because people were frequently customizing Bugzilla at their company – and it was an unreadable, garbled mess.

Thankfully, both of those problems had the same solution. The performance problem was solved by allowing people to run Bugzilla in a way that would pre-compile all the code when the web server started, instead of every time somebody loaded a page. And to enable that pre-compiling, we had to do enormous amounts of refactoring. So, we actually ended up handling our performance problem *by* handling our code problem.

However, it took *four major releases* (Bugzilla 2.18, 2.20, 2.22, and finally 3.0) to get all this done! We fixed a lot of little issues for each release along the way, too, so each release really did suck less than the previous one. But handling the major issues was a tremendous effort – it wasn't just something we could code up in one night and have it be done with.

> **Sometimes the big issues in a software project don't get handled because they *do* require that much work to fix. This doesn't mean you can ignore them, it just means that you have to plan for a long project, and figure out how you can keep getting releases out in the meantime.**

After all that was fixed, then we could turn our attention elsewhere, and wow! It turned out that elsewhere, there were still a bunch of things that sucked! All of the sudden, there were a new batch of "totally obvious" things to fix – things that had been there all the time, but were just overshadowed by the previous set of "totally obvious" things.

Now, we could have just gone on like this forever — fixing one set of "totally obvious" problems and then going on to the next set of "totally obvious" problems. But we ran into an issue — what happens when suddenly, you get to the point where there are *fifty* "totally obvious" things that need fixing, and you can't get them all done for one release? Well, that's when you suddenly need some method of prioritizing what you're going to fix.

For the Bugzilla Project, there were two things that we did that *really* helped us prioritize:

1. **The Bugzilla Survey**: `https://wiki.mozilla.org/Bugzilla:Survey`

2. **The Bugzilla Usability Study**: `https://wiki.mozilla.org/Bugzilla:CMU_HCI_Research_2008`

With the survey, the most important part was allowing people to respond in free-form text, to questions asked to *them personally*. That is, I sent the questions from me personally to Bugzilla administrators personally, often customizing the message for their exact situation. And there were no multiple-choice questions, only questions that prompted them to tell us what was bothering them and what they wanted to see. They were actually really happy to get my emails — lots of them thanked me for just doing the survey.

Once they had all responded, I read everything and compiled a list of major issues that were reported — overall a surprisingly small list! We're focusing on those issues pretty heavily nowadays, and I think it's making people happier with Bugzilla in general.

With the usability study, surprisingly the most helpful part was when the researchers (who were usability experts) just sat down in front of Bugzilla and pointed out things that violated usability principles. That is, even more valuable than the actual *research* they did was just *their observations* as experts, using the standard principles of usability engineering. The fact that they were fresh eyes – people who'd never worked on Bugzilla and thus didn't just think "well that's the way it is" – also was important, I think.

So we took all this data, and it really helped us prioritize. However, it's important that we did the survey and research *when we did them* and not earlier. Back before we fixed the top few major issues, the usability and survey results would have just been overwhelming to us – they would have pointed out a million things we already knew, or a lot of things that we just didn't have the time to work on at that point, and we would have had to re-do the survey and research again later, making it all a bunch of wasted time. So we had to wait until we were at the point of asking ourselves, "Okay, what's most important now?", and that was when gathering data became tremendously important and incredibly useful.

> **So overall, I'd say that when you're trying to make things suck less, first go with what you *know* are the top few big obvious issues, and handle those, no matter what it takes.**

Then things will calm down a little, and you'll have a huge pile of stuff that all needs fixing. That's when you go and *gather data* from your users, and work to fix whatever they tell you actually sucks.

-Max

∾ 35 ∾

THE POWER
OF NO

How many times have you used a piece of software that was full of incredibly convoluted features, strange decisions, and unusable interfaces? Have you ever wanted to physically or verbally abuse a computer because it just wouldn't do things right, or you couldn't figure out how to make it function properly? And how often have you thought, "How could any programmer think this was a sane idea?"

Well if you've ever experienced any of those things, your next thought might have been something like "**** this computer" or "**** the silly programmer who made it behave this way". After all, aren't programmers and hardware designers to blame for the crazy behavior of the system? Well, yes, to some extent they are. But after being intimately involved in software design for many years, I now have another reaction to poorly-implemented features. Instead of becoming angry with the programmer who implemented the system, I ask myself, "Who was the software designer who *authorized* this feature?" Who stood by silently and let this feature happen when they had the power to stop it?

Granted, sometimes there is no software designer at all, in which case you're practically guaranteed to have a broken system. But when there is a software designer, they are ultimately responsible for how the system is put together. Now, quite a bit of this job involves designing the structure of features before they go into the system. But there's also another part of the job of a software designer – preventing bad ideas from being implemented. In fact, if there's any lesson I've learned from my years in the software industry, it's this:

> **The most important word in a software designer's vocabulary is "no".**

The problem is that if you give a group of humans total freedom to implement any random idea that comes into their mind, then nearly every time they will implement bad ideas. This isn't a criticism of developers, it's more of a fact of life. I have great faith in the intelligence and capability of individual developers. I admire developers' struggles and achievements in software development. It's just an unfortunate fact of existence that without some central guidance, people in a group tend to evolve complex systems that don't help their users as well as they could.

An individual designer, however, is usually capable of creating a consistent and enjoyable experience for the users and developers both. But if that individual designer never steps up and say "no" when another developer starts to do something the wrong way, then the system will collapse on itself and become a chaotic mess of bad ideas. So it is very important to have a software designer who has the power to say "no", and then it's important for that designer to actually *use* that power whenever it is appropriate.

It is truly amazing how much you can improve your product just by saying "no" to any idea that really deserves a "no".

Recognizing Bad Ideas

Before you can apply this principle, there is one thing that you have to know: how to recognize bad ideas. Thankfully, there are a lot of software design principles that help clue you in on what is a bad idea, and lead you to saying "no" when it's truly needed. For example:

♦ If the implementation of the feature violates the laws of software design (for example, it's too complex, it can't be maintained, it won't be easily changeable, etc.) then that implementation is a bad idea.

♦ If the feature doesn't help the users, it's a bad idea.

♦ If the proposal is *obviously stupid*, it's a bad idea.

♦ If some change doesn't fix a proven problem, it's a bad idea.

♦ If you aren't certain that it's a good idea, it's a bad idea.

Also, one tends to learn over time what is and isn't a good idea, particularly if you use the above as guidelines and understand the laws of software design.

Having No Better Idea

Now, sometimes a designer *can* recognize a bad idea, but they still implement it because they can't think of a better idea right now. This is a mistake. If you can think up only one solution to a problem but it is obviously stupid, then you *still need to say no to it*.

At first this may seem counter-intuitive – don't problems need to be solved? Shouldn't we solve this problem in any way we can?

Well, here's the problem: if you implement a "bad idea", your "solution" will rapidly become a worse disaster than the original problem ever was. When you implement something terrible, it "works", but the users complain, the other programmers all sigh, the system is broken, and the popularity of your software starts to decrease. Eventually, the "solution" becomes such a problem that it requires *other* bad "solutions" to "fix" it. These "fixes" then become enormous problems in themselves. Continue down this path, and eventually you end up with a system that is bloated, confused, and difficult to maintain, just like many existing software systems today.

If you often find yourself in a situation where you feel forced to accept bad ideas, it's likely that you're actually near the *end* of this chain of events – that is, you're actually building on a series of *pre-existing* bad ideas from the system's past. In that case, the solution is not to keep "patching" over the bad ideas, but to instead find the most fundamental, underlying bad ideas of the system and redesign them to be good, over time.

Now *ideally*, when you reject a bad idea, you should provide an alternate, good idea in its place — that way you're being constructive and moving the project forward, instead of being viewed as a roadblock on the path of development. But even if you *can't* come up with a better idea right now, it's still important to say no to bad ideas. A good idea *will come* eventually. Maybe it will take some study, or perhaps it will suddenly come to you while you're standing in the shower one day. I have no idea where the idea will come from or what it will be. But don't worry too much about it. Just trust that there is *always* some good way to solve every problem, and keep looking for it until you find it. Don't give up and accept bad ideas.

Clarification: Acceptance and Politeness

So it's important to say "no", but there are a few clarifications required on what I really mean, there. I'm not saying that every suggestion is wrong. In fact, developers are usually very bright people, and sometimes they really do nail it. Many developers make perfect suggestions and do excellent implementations. And even the worst solutions can have good parts, despite not being excellent as a whole.

> **So many times, instead of actually saying "no", what you'll be saying is something more like, "Wow, there's a part of this idea that *is* really good, but the rest of it is not so great.**

We should take the best parts of this idea and build them up into something awesome by doing more work on them." You *do* have say no to the parts of an idea that are bad, though. Just because one part of the idea is good doesn't mean that the whole idea is good. Take what's intelligent about the idea, refine it, and build good ideas around it until the solution you've designed really is great.

Also, it is still critically important that you communicate *well* with the rest of your team – having the responsibility of saying "no" doesn't give you the right to be rude or inconsiderate. If you continuously say "no" without any hint of kindness, you are going to fracture your team, cause upsets, and ultimately end up wasting hours of your time in argument with the people you've upset.

So when you have to say "no", it's best to find a polite way to communicate it – a way that expresses appreciation for the input, positive suggestions of how to improve things, and lets the person down easily. I understand how frustrating it can be to have to slow down and explain things – and even *more* frustrating to repeat the explanation over and over to somebody who doesn't get it the first time – but if that's what it takes to have an effective development team while still saying "no" to bad features, then that's what you have to do.

-Max

∽ 36 ∽

WHY PROGRAMMERS SUCK

A long time ago, I wrote an essay called "*Why Computers Suck*" (it was given the title "*Computers*" and "*What's Wrong With Computers*" in two later revisions, and the original title never saw the light of day). The article was fairly long, but it basically came down to the idea that computers suck because programmers create crazy complicated stuff that nobody else can understand, and complexity builds on complexity until every aspect of a program becomes unmanageable.

What I *didn't* know at the time was *why* programmers did this. It was obvious that they *did* do it, but why would the software development industry produce so *many* crazy, complex masses of unreadable code? Why did it *keep happening*, even when developers should have learned their lesson after their first bad experience?

> **What was it that made programmers not just make bad code, but keep on making bad code?**

Well, this was a mystery, but I didn't worry too much about it at first. Just the revelation that "bad programs are caused entirely by bad programmers", as simple and obvious as it may seem, was enough to fuel an entire investigation and study into the field of programming, one which had some pretty good results. The problem had been defined (bad programmers who create complexity), and the problem seemed to have a solution (describe laws of software design that would prevent this); so that was enough for me.

But it still baffled me that the world's universities, technical schools, and training programs could turn out such terrible programmers, even with all of the decades of advancement in software development techniques. Sure, a lot of the principles of software design hadn't been codified, but a lot of good advice was floating around, a lot of it very common. Even if people hadn't gone to school, didn't they *read* any of this advice?

Well, the truth was beyond my imagination, and it took almost five years of working on the Bugzilla Project with a vast number of separate contributors until one day I suddenly realized an appalling fact:

> **The vast majority (90% or more) of programmers have absolutely no idea what they are doing.**

It's not that these programmers haven't read about software design (though they likely haven't). It's not that the programming languages are too complex (though they are). It's that the vast majority of programmers don't have the first clue what they are really doing. They are just mimicking the mistakes of other programmers – copying code and typing more-or-less meaningless incantations at the machine, in the hope that it would behave like they wanted. All of this without any real understanding of the mechanics of the computer, the principles of software design, or the meanings of each individual word and symbol they were typing into the computer.

That is a bold, shocking, and offensive statement, but it has held up in my experience. I have personally reviewed and given feedback on the code of scores of programmers. I have read the code of many others. I have talked to many, many programmers about software development, and I've read the writings of hundreds of developers.

> **The number of programmers who really understand what they are doing comprise only about 10% of all the programmers I've ever talked to, worked with, or heard about.**

In open source, we get the cream of the crop – people who want to program in their spare time. And even then, I'd say only about 20% of open source programmers have a really good handle on what they are doing.

So why is this? What's the problem? How could there be so many people working in this field who have absolutely no clue what they're doing?

Well, that sounds a bit like they're somehow "stupid." But what *is* stupidity? People are not stupid simply for *not knowing* something. There's a lot of stuff that *everybody* doesn't know. That doesn't make them stupid. That may make them *ignorant* about certain things, but it doesn't make them stupid.

No, stupidity, real stupidity, is *not knowing that you don't know.* Stupid people *think they know something when they don't,* or they *have no idea that there is something more to know.*

> **This sort of stupidity is something that can be found in nearly every field, and software development is no exception.**

Many programmers simply don't know that there *could be* laws or general guidelines for software development, and so they don't even go looking for them. At many software companies, there's no attempt to improve developers' understanding of the programming language they're using – perhaps simply because they think that the programmers must "already know it if they were hired to do it".

Unfortunately, it's particularly harmful to have this sort of mindset in software development, because there is *so much to know* if you really want to be good. Anybody who thinks they already know everything (or who has a "blind spot" where they can't see that there's more to learn) is having their ability to produce excellent code crippled by a lack of knowledge – knowledge they *don't even know exists* and that they *don't even know they lack.*

No matter how much you know, there is almost always more to know about *any* field, and computer programming is no exception. So it's always wrong to think you know everything.

What to Study

Sometimes it's hard to figure out *what* one should be learning about, though. There's so much data, where does one start? Well, to help you out, I've come up with a few questions you can ask yourself or others to help figure out what areas might need more study:

♦ Do you know as much as possible about every single word and symbol on every page of code you're writing?

♦ Did you read and completely understand the documentation of every single function you're using?

♦ Do you have an excellent grasp of the fundamental principles of software development – such a good grasp that you could explain them flawlessly to novice programmers at your organization?

♦ Do you understand how each component of the computer functions, and how they all work together?

♦ Do you understand the history of computers, and where they're going in the future, so that you can understand how your code will function on the computers that will be built in the future?

♦ Do you know the history of programming languages, so that you can understand how the language you're using evolved and *why* it works like it does?

♦ Do you understand other programming languages, other methods of programming, and other types of computers than the one you're using, so that you know what the *actual* best tool for each job is?

> **From top to bottom, those are the most important things for any programmer to know about the code they're writing. If you can truthfully answer "yes" to all those questions, then you are an excellent programmer.**

It may seem like an overwhelming study list to you. "Wow, the documentation for *every single function*? Reading that is going to take too long!" Well, you know what else takes a long time? Becoming a good programmer if you *don't* read the documentation. You know how long it takes? *Forever*, because it never happens.

You will *never* become a good programmer simply by copying other people's code and praying that it works right for you. But even more importantly, investing time into *learning* is what it takes to become good. Taking the time *now* will make you a *much* faster programmer later. If you spend a lot of time reading up on stuff for the first three months that you're learning a new technology, you'll probably be 10 times faster with it for the next 10 years than if you'd just dived into it and then never read anything at all.

I do want to put a certain limiter on that, though – you can't *just* read for three months and expect to become a good programmer. First of all, that's just too boring – nobody wants to just study theory for three months and not get any actual practice in. Very few people would keep up with that for long enough to become programmers at all, let alone good programmers. So I want to point out that understanding comes also from *practice*, not just from study. But *without the study*, understanding may *never* come. So it's important to balance both the study and the practice of programming.

This is not an attack on any programmer that I've worked with personally, or even an attack on any individual programmer at all. I admire almost every programmer I've ever known, as a person, and I expect I'd admire the rest were I to meet them, as well.

Instead, this is an open invitation to *all* programmers to open your mind to the thought that there might always be more to know, that both knowledge and practice are the key to skill, and that it's not shameful at all to *not know* something – as long as you *know* that you don't know it, and take the time to learn it when necessary.

-Max

∼ 37 ∼

THE SECRET OF FAST PROGRAMMING: STOP THINKING

When I talk to developers about code complexity, they often say that they *want* to write simple code, but deadline pressure or underlying issues mean that they just don't have the time or knowledge necessary to both complete the task and refine it to simplicity.

Well, it's certainly true that putting time pressure on developers tends to lead to them writing complex code. However, deadlines don't *have* to lead to complexity. Instead of saying "This deadline prevents me from writing simple code," one could equally say, "I am not a fast-enough programmer to make this simple." That is, the faster you are as a programmer, the less your code quality has to be affected by deadlines.

Now, that's nice to say, but how does one actually *become* faster? Is it a magic skill that people are born with? Do you become fast by being somehow "smarter" than other people?

No, it's not magic or in-born at all. In fact, there is just one simple rule that, if followed, will eventually solve the problem entirely:

> **Any time you find yourself stopping to think, something is wrong.**

Perhaps that sounds incredible, but it works remarkably well. Think about it – when you're sitting in front of your editor but not coding very quickly, is it because you're a slow typer? I doubt it – "having to type too much" is rarely a developer's productivity problem.

Instead, the pauses where you're *not* typing are what make it slow. And what are developers usually doing during those pauses? Stopping to think – perhaps about the problem, perhaps about the tools, perhaps about email, whatever. But any time this happens, it indicates a problem.

The thinking is not the problem itself – it is a *sign* of some other problem. It could be one of the many different issues that we're going to look at now.

Understanding

Just the other day it was taking me hours to write what should have been a really simple service. I kept stopping to think about it, trying to work out how it should behave. Finally, I realized that I didn't understand one of the input variables to the primary function. I knew the *name* of its type, but I had never gone and read the definition of the type – I didn't really *understand* what that variable (a word or symbol) meant.

The most common reason developers stop to think is that they did not fully understand some word or symbol.

As soon as I looked up the type's code and docs, everything became clear and I wrote that service like a *demon* (pun partially intended).

This can happen in almost infinite ways. Many people dive into a programming language without learning what (,), [,], {, }, +, *, and % really mean in that language. Some developers don't understand how the computer really works.

When you truly understand, you don't have to stop to think. That was also a major motivation behind my first book, *Code Simplicity* – when you understand that there are unshakable laws to software design, that can eliminate a lot of the "stopping to think" moments.

So if you find that you are stopping to think, don't try to solve the problem in your mind – search outside of yourself for what you didn't understand. Then go *look* at something that will help you understand it.

This even applies to questions like "Will a user ever read this text?" You might not have a User Experience Research Department to really answer that question, but you can at least make a drawing, show it to somebody, and ask their opinion. Don't just sit there and think – *do something*. Only action leads to understanding.

Drawing

Sometimes developers stop to think because they can't hold enough concepts in their mind at once – lots of things are relating to each other in a complex way and they have to think through it. In this case, it's almost always more efficient to write or draw something than it is to think about it.

What you want is something you can *look* at, or somehow perceive outside of yourself. This is a form of understanding, but it's special enough that I wanted to call it out on its own.

Starting

Sometimes the problem is "I have no idea what code to start writing." The simplest solution here is to just start writing whatever code you know that you *can* write right now. Pick the part of the problem that you understand *completely*, and write the solution for that — even if it's just one function, or an unimportant class.

> **Often, the simplest piece of code to start with is the "core" of the application.**

For example, if I was going to write a YouTube app, I would start with the video player. Think of it as an exercise in continuous delivery — write the code that would actually make a *product* first, no matter how silly or small that product is. A video player without any other UI is a product that does something useful (play video), even if it's not a *complete* product yet.

> **If you're not sure how to write even that core code yet, then just start with the code you are sure about.**

Generally I find that once a piece of the problem becomes solved, it's much easier to solve the rest of it. Sometimes the problem unfolds in steps — you solve one part, which makes the solution of the next part obvious, and so forth. Whichever part doesn't require much thinking to create, write that part now.

Skipping a Step

Another specialized understanding problem is when you've skipped some step in the proper sequence of development. For example, let's say our Bike object depends on the Wheels, Pedals, and Frame objects. If you try to write the whole Bike object without writing the Wheels, Pedals, or Frame objects, you're going to have to *think* a lot about those non-existent classes. On the other hand, if you write the Wheels class when there is no Bike class at all, you might have to think a lot about how the Wheels class is going to be used by the Bike class.

> **Don't jump over steps in the development of your system and expect that you'll be productive.**

The right approach in the example above, would be to implement enough of the Bike class to get to the point where you need Wheels. Then write enough of the Wheels class to satisfy your immediate need in the Bike class. Then go back to the Bike class, and work on that until the next time you need one of the underlying pieces. So just as I suggested earlier, find the part of the problem that you can solve without thinking, and solve that immediately.

Physical Problems

If I haven't eaten enough, I tend to get distracted and start to think because I'm hungry. It might not be thoughts *about* my stomach, but I *wouldn't* be thinking if I were full – I'd be focused. This can also happen with sleep, illness, or any sort of body problem.

It's not as common as the "understanding" problem from above, so first always look for something you didn't fully understand. If you're really sure you understood *everything*, then physical problems could be a candidate.

Distractions

When a developer becomes distracted by something external, such as noise, it can take some thinking to remember where they were in their solution. The answer here is relatively simple – before you start to develop, make sure that you are in an environment that will not distract you, or make it impossible for distractions to interrupt you.

Some people close the door to their office, some people put on headphones, some people put up a "do not disturb" sign – whatever it takes. You might have to work together with your manager or co-workers to create a truly distraction-free environment for development.

Self-Doubt

Sometimes a developer sits and thinks because they feel unsure about themselves or their decisions. The solution to this is similar to the solution in the "*Understanding*" section – whatever you are uncertain about, learn more about it until you become certain enough to write code.

If you just feel generally uncertain as a programmer, it might be that there are *many* things to learn more about, such as the study fundamentals that I listed in *Chapter 36, Why Programmers Suck*. Go through each piece you need to study until you really understand it, then move on to the next piece, and so on.

There will always be learning involved in the process of programming, but as you know more and more about it, you will become faster and faster and have to think less and less.

False Ideas

Many people have been told that thinking is what smart people do, thus, they stop to think in order to make intelligent decisions. However, this is a false idea. If thinking alone made you a genius, then *everybody* would be Einstein.

Truly smart people learn, observe, decide, and act. They gain knowledge and then use that knowledge to address the problems in front of them. If you really want to be smart, use your intelligence to cause action in the physical universe – don't use it just to think great thoughts to yourself.

Caveat

All of the above is the secret to being a fast programmer *when you are sitting and writing code*. If you are caught up all day in reading email and going to meetings, then no programming happens whatsoever – that's a different problem.

Still, there are some analogous solutions you could try. Perhaps the organization does not fully understand you or your role, which is why they're sending you so much email and putting you in so many meetings. Perhaps there's something about the organization that you don't fully understand, such as how to go to fewer meetings and get less email. Maybe even some organizational difficulties can be resolved by adapting the solutions in this post to groups of people instead of individuals.

-Max

～38～

DEVELOPER HUBRIS

Your program is not important to me. I don't care about its user interface. I don't care what its name is. I don't care that you made it, or what version it is.

The only thing I care about is that your program helps me accomplish my purpose. That's a truly remarkable feat, and if your program does it, you should be proud. There's no need to make your program take up more of my attention just because you think it's important.

Now of course, your program is important to you! When you work on code for a long time, it's easy to become attached to it. It was so hard to write. Your cleverness is unbounded, shadowing lesser mortals in the mountain of your intellect. You have overcome some of the greatest mental obstacles man has ever faced. Truly, you must shout this from the tops of every tower, through the streets of every city, and even unto the caves of the Earth. **But don't**.

Because your users *do not care*. Your fellow developers might be interested, but your users are *not*.

> **When you're truly clever, what will show up for users is that your program is awesome. It's so awesome, the user hardly notices it's there. That is true brilliance.**

The worst offenders against this ideal are programs that pop up a window every time my computer starts. I know your software is there. I installed it. You really don't need to remind me. If my purpose is to start up my computer so I can use it, how is your pop up window helping me accomplish that? It's not, so get rid of it.

There are smaller ways to cause problems, too, that all revolve around asking for too much time or attention from the user:

♦ "Users will definitely be okay with clicking through three screens of forms before they can use my product."

♦ "I'm sure that users will want to learn all the icons I *invented* for this program, so taking away the text labels for those icons is fine!"

♦ "I'm sure it's okay to stop the user from working by popping up these dialog boxes."

♦ "Users will totally want to search through this huge page for a tiny little piece of text so they can click on it."

♦ "Why should we make this simpler? That would be a lot of work, and it's already pretty easy...for me."

And so on.

The true humility required of a developer is the willingness to remove their identity from the user's world.

Stop telling the user the program is there. Don't think that the user cares about your program, wants to spend time using its interface, or wants to learn about it. It's not your program that they care about — it's their *purpose*. Help them accomplish that perfectly, and you will have created the perfect program for them.

-Max

~ 39 ~

"Consistency" Does Not Mean "Uniformity"

In a user interface, similar things should look the same. But *different* things should look **different**.

Why did over 75% of Facebook's users think that the May 2009 Facebook UI redesign was bad? Because it made *different* things look *similar* to each other. Nobody could tell if they were updating their status or writing on somebody else's wall, because even though the text was slightly different in the box depending on what you were doing, the box itself *looked the same*. Similarly, the new Chat UI (introduced a few days later) made idle users look basically identical to active users, except for a tiny icon difference. (It's also important that different things are different *enough*, not just a little different, because people often won't notice little differences.)

> **This is an easy pitfall for developers to fall into because developers love consistency.**

Everything should be based on a single framework, in the backend of an application. But that doesn't mean that everything has to be displayed the same in the UI.

This fact – that different things should look different – is actually true with code, too, but people rarely think about it, because developers are actually pretty good about it. For example, accessing a value of an object should look different than calling a method on it, and in most programs, it does.

For example, in Bugzilla's code, accessing a value on an object looks like `$object->value` whereas calling a method on the object looks like `$object->method()`. It's not all *that* different, but the `()` at the end is enough difference for the average programmer to notice "Oh, that's a method call that *does something* – it's not just accessing a value in the object."

All in all, consistency is really important in both the backend and the frontend of an application. But that doesn't mean that every single thing should look exactly the same. If we took that to extremes, we'd just have a solid white page, and that doesn't seem all that usable (frontend) or readable (backend), does it?

-Max

~ 40 ~

USERS HAVE PROBLEMS, DEVELOPERS HAVE SOLUTIONS

In the world of software, it is the job of software developers to solve the problems of users. Users present a problem, and the developers solve it. Whenever these roles are reversed, trouble ensues.

If you ever want to see a bloated, useless, complex piece of software, find one where the developers implemented every solution that any user ever suggested. It's true that the users are the people who know what the problem is, and that sometimes, they have novel ideas for solutions. But the people making the final decision on how a problem is to be solved should always be the developers of the system, not its users.

This problem can be particularly bad when you're writing software for a small number of users internally at an organization. The users who you are writing for often have inordinate power over you, by virtue of being executives or being close to executives. They can, quite literally, tell you what to do. However, if they want a solution that is *actually* good for them, they should try to refrain from this practice.

Trust and Information

If you trust a team enough to have them write software for you, then you should also trust them enough to make decisions about that software. If you don't trust them, why are they working at your organization?

A group of people who distrust each other is usually a highly inefficient group – perhaps not even really a "group" at all, but merely a collection of individuals all trying to defend themselves from each other. That's no way to run an organization or to have anybody in it lead a happy life.

If a user wants to influence a developer's decision, the best thing they can do is offer *data*. Developers need information in order to make good decisions for their users, and that information often comes from the users themselves.

If you as a user think that a piece of software is going the wrong direction, provide information about the problem that you would like solved, and explain why the current software doesn't solve it. Get information about how many other people have this problem. The best is if you can show numbers, but sometimes even anecdotes can be helpful when a developer is trying to make a decision. Developers should judge data appropriately (hard data about lots of users is obviously better than an anecdote from a single user) but they usually appreciate all the information given to them when it's offered as data and not as a demand for a specific solution.

Problems Come from Users

Developers, on the other hand, often have the opposite problem. If you want to see a piece of software that users hate, find one where the developers simply *imagined* that the users had a problem, and then started developing a solution for that problem.

> **Problems come from *users*, not from developers.**

Sometimes the developers of a piece of software are also users of it, and they can see obvious problems that they themselves are experiencing. That's fine, but they should offer that up as *data*, from the viewpoint of a *user*, and make sure that it's something that other people are also actually experiencing. Developers should treat their own opinions as somewhat more valuable than the average user's (because they see lots of user feedback and they work with their program day in and day out) but still as *an opinion that came from a user*.

> **When you solve the developers' problems instead of the users' problems, you're putting lots of effort into something that isn't going to help people in the best possible way.**

It may be enjoyable to assert one's opinion, be the smartest person in the room, and cause the team to solve your problem, but it feels terrible to release software that ends up not helping people.

Also, I usually find that solving the developers' problems leads to a lot more complexity than solving the users' problems. So it would actually have been *easier* to find out from the user what was wrong and fix that, rather than imagine a problem and grind away at it.

Now, I'm not saying that no developer has ever come up with a valid problem, and that no user has ever come up with a valid solution. Sometimes these things do happen. But the *judgment* about these things should lie on the appropriate sides of the equation.

Only users (and preferably, a large number of them, or data about a large number of them) can truly tell you what problem they are experiencing, and only somebody on the development side (preferably, an individual who is tasked with making this decision after understanding the problem and possibly getting feedback from his peers) can correctly decide which solution should be implemented.

-Max

~ 41 ~

INSTANT GRATIFICATION = INSTANT FAILURE

The broadest problem that I see in the software industry is that companies are unwilling to engage in strategies that only show results in the long term. Or, more specifically, that organizations are unaware that there *is* any such thing as a long-term strategy.

In the US, it's probably a symptom of a general cultural problem – if an American can't see an instant result from something, they think it doesn't work. This leads to fast food, french fries, and obesity. The healthy way to eat (protein and vegetables) has a *delayed* effect on the body (you don't get the energy for over an hour), and the bad way to eat (endless carbohydrates without nutritional value) has an instant result – immediate energy.

Software is always a long-term process.

I wrote the first version of VCI (`https://metacpan.org/pod/VCI`), in about three weeks, and that was *insanely fast*. Any actual application (VCI is just a library for interacting with version-control systems), takes months or years of person-hours, even if you keep it small. So you'd think that organizations would be far-sighted about their development strategies, right?

Unfortunately, it just doesn't happen. Competitor X comes out with "Shiny New Feature" and The Company says "We must have Shiny New Feature RIGHT NOW!"

That's not a long-term winning strategy, that's just short-sighted panic. If you have users, they're not all going to get up and go away in the next five minutes just because somebody else has one feature that you don't. You should be looking at *trends* of how many users you're gaining or losing, not just responding mindlessly to the immediate environment.

Solving for the long term

So what's a good long-term strategy? Well, refactoring your code so that you will still be able to add features in the future, that's a good one. Or spending some extra time putting some polish on your features and UI so that when the product is released, users are actually happy with it. *Not* adding features that you don't want to maintain, if they're not important enough – that's another one.

Remember that Mozilla (`http://www.mozilla.org`) did poorly for years, only to finally start gaining dominance in a market that Netscape had lost, because they had a *long-term* plan. Granted, Mozilla made some decisions early on that caused some things to take longer than they should have, but they still won out in the long term, despite failing in the short term.

Of course, it can be hard to convince people that your long-term plan is right, sometimes, because it takes so long to show results! When I started refactoring Bugzilla (`https://www.bugzilla.org/`) in 2004 there was pretty constant resistance, particularly when I would review patches and say, "You need to wait for the new architecture before this can go in," or "This needs to be fixed to not be spaghetti code."

But once the refactoring really got rolling (after about two and a half years), it suddenly became way easier to add new features and nearly all the developers became big supporters of refactoring.

How to Ruin Your Software Company

I've read a lot of so-called advice on "how to run your software business" that just focuses on instant gratification – what you can get done *right now*. Add features! Get millions of dollars instantly from VCs! Unfortunately, the way the universe seems to work is that you can destroy something in an instant, but **it takes time to create something**.

So in reality, the closer you get to "instant gratification", the closer you get to destruction of your product, your business, and your future.

So here's a key lesson for the software industry:

> **If you want a good plan, pick one that admits that creation takes time. It doesn't have to take forever, but it's never instant.**

-Max

~42~

SUCCESS COMES FROM EXECUTION, NOT INNOVATION

There's a strange sort of social disease going around in technology circles today, which centers around this word "innovation."

Everybody wants to "innovate." The news talks about "who's being the most innovative." Marketing for companies insists that they are "innovating."

> **Except actually, it's not innovation that leads to success. It's *execution*.**

It doesn't matter how good or how new my idea is. It matters how well I carry it out in the real world.

Now, our history books worship the inventors, not the executors. We are taught all about the people who invent new things, come up with new ideas, and plough new trails. But look around you in present time and in the recent past, and you'll see that the most successful people are the ones who *carried out the idea really well*, not the people who came up with the idea.

Elvis didn't invent rock and roll. Ford didn't invent the automobile *or* the assembly line. Apple didn't invent the GUI. Webster didn't invent dictionaries. Maytag didn't invent the washing machine. Google didn't invent web searching. I could go on and on and **on**.

Granted, sometimes the innovator also is an excellent executor, but usually that's not the case. Most inventors don't turn out to be the most successful people in their field (or even successful at all).

So stop worrying about "coming up with something new." You don't have to do that. You just have to execute an *already existing* idea really, really well. You can add your own flair to it, maybe, or fix it up a little, but you don't have to have something brand new.

There are so many examples that prove this that it's hard *not* to see one if you move your eyes *anywhere*. Just look, you'll see.

Now, I'm not saying that people shouldn't innovate. You should! It's fun, and it advances the whole human race a tiny step every time you do. But it's not the path to long-term success for you or for any group you belong to. That's all in execution.

-Max

~ 43 ~

EXCELLENT
SOFTWARE

Note: This is one of the first articles that I ever wrote. Some of the other data in this book and in my book and my blog, Code Simplicity, are in fact based on some of the principles in this chapter. However, it has never been published anywhere before now. Enjoy.

A truly excellent program **carries out the user's intention exactly as they intended it**.

If you want to break it down a bit more, this means that an excellent program:

1. Does exactly what the user told it to do.

2. Behaves exactly like the user expects it to behave.

3. Does not block the user from communicating their intention.

To be truly excellent, software must do all of those things. Think of any piece of software that average users truly enjoy using, and you'll find it satisfies those three criteria.

There is an odd feeling of satisfaction that comes from the computer carrying out your intentions perfectly. And this is one of the joys of programming – when the computer does exactly what you intended, it's very satisfying. So let's now examine these three aspects in turn.

1. Does exactly what the user told it to do

Obviously, this is the primary key to carrying out the user's intention. They told us to do something, so we do it.

A program shouldn't do surprising things. When you tell a program to send an email, the program should just *send the email*. It shouldn't also clean your socks, remind you to turn off the oven, and pay your taxes.

Also, if at any time you don't do exactly what the user told you to do, you must inform them. You should minimize these occurrences, because *any* time a program doesn't do what the user told it to do (even for reasons outside the control of the program), that detracts from the user's opinion of the excellence of the software. In our above example, the program shouldn't fail to send the email without informing the user that it failed. Failing is not what the user told it to do, and so the user needs to know.

The email example seems obvious, but there are many less obvious examples in the world of computing.

> **Programmers often debate whether or not a program should report an error, or if it should do other things, when the user has only told it to do one thing. The answer is the answer to the question: what did the user tell us to do?**

Remember, if the user has set some preferences, that's also an instruction to the program. So preferences are a perfectly valid way of deciding "what did the user tell us to do." Adding lots of preferences to a program increases complexity, though, so it's not the best solution to most problems.

2. Behaves exactly like the user expects it to behave

The user's intention is expressed through things like mouse clicks and keyboard input. This isn't the most perfect method of communication, so sometimes we have to do a little guessing.

> **This particular rule means that your program should respond to the user's input in the way the user expects it to respond. Which means that it acts like other things the user has used in the past, or it acts exactly like the documentation says it acts.**

Note that I didn't say "other programs the user has used in the past." I said, "other things." Users have used doors in real life, so if your program has a door in it, users expect it to open and close when they push on it or turn the handle. They expect that when the door is open, things can go "through" it, and when the door is closed, things can't go through it.

It is also true for "other programs," though. Users know what a "scrollbar" is because other programs have scrollbars. Users know what a keyboard is because every computer has one, and because they learned all the letters of their alphabet somewhere. (But if you make a keyboard with a button called "Qfwfq" then you'd better have some easy-to-read documentation explaining the "Qfwfq" button.)

Generally, the most excellent software avoids making the user ever read the documentation. They know everything about this program because it behaves just like other programs, behaves like other things they've experienced in real life, or there's text right inside the program itself that explains things. (Beware that many users don't read text, but that's starting to get into a whole other subject called "Human-Computer Interaction" and this is not a book on Human-Computer Interaction.)

This can, once in a while, conflict with "do exactly what the user told us to do." Sometimes the user expects a program to do something they didn't say to do. For example, I usually expect an email program to save my sent messages somewhere, even if I haven't told it to.

If there is a conflict between this rule and "do exactly what the user told us to do," and you're in doubt about which way to go, always just do what the user told us to do. You should only violate the "do what the user told us" rule when you're sure the user has some expectation that violates the rule.

The best software behaves exactly like you expect it to behave, and never does anything you didn't tell it to do.

3. Does not block the user from communicating their intention

If the user is unable to communicate their intention to your program, your program has failed the most basic requirement for carrying out the user's intention – the user actually being able to *communicate* that intention. Primarily, this requirement can be translated into "The program should be **simple to use**."

> **You should make it easy as humanly possible for the user to communicate their intention to your program.**

The simpler your program is to use, the more likely it is that the user will be able to determine how to communicate their intention. If you have made it too difficult for a user to communicate their intention, then you have blocked them. Any time the user fails to communicate their intention, it is most likely because it was too difficult for them to communicate it.

I know for a fact that people with an IQ of 75 can use Notepad. That is simple enough. So we should never be saying "My users are stupid." We should be saying "I haven't yet figured out how to make my program simple enough for my users to use."

"Simple," in the context of interacting with a program, means "allows the user to easily and quickly do what they want, with the way of doing it presented in an obvious manner".

The "obvious" part is usually more important than the "easily and quickly" part. If somebody has to go through three steps to do something, but they're three steps that are made very clear and obvious by the program, that's *simple*, from the user's perspective. However, the ideal of "simple" is "happens instantly, in one step, with one obvious command to the computer." On most computers, the simplest operation is turning them on. (Some computers manage to make even that complex, though.)

Ideally, most actions on a computer should be as simple as the power button is.

If the user can't figure out how to do something, your program might as well just not do it at all. If it's harder to use a program than to do a task manually, then people will do the task manually instead of using the program.

There is a lot of software that specific people (like programmers) enjoy using but others don't. This is because to the advanced user, that program is simple to use, but to other people, it isn't. So obviously, how "simple" you need to be is relative to who your users are going to be. But the simpler you make the program, the more people will find it excellent.

Even programmers can use simple programs, if that program does exactly what they need to do, exactly how they need to do it. Most complex programs that only advanced users use are *in* use because nobody has thought up a way to make them simple yet.

However, remember that simplicity doesn't involve doing lots of things the user didn't tell you to do! One button that does ten things simultaneously might not be simple and might not be excellent software.

Excellence is senior to (but is not in conflict with) code simplicity

Nothing I have ever written excuses you from writing excellent software. If you have to add some tiny bit of complexity to the internals of your program in order to make it excellent, you should do that. Adding complexity to the user interface almost never makes your program excellent, though. (That violates "simple to use.")

I'd say that 99.9% of the time, simplicity and following the principles of software design will lead to excellent software, and you should only violate a software design rule when you're certain that's the only way to deliver excellence.

-Max

INDEX

A

action 155

B

backwards-compatibility 25, 27
bad ideas
    recognizing 215
barriers
    removing 137, 139
bug
    clarifying 79-84
    compound complexity 66
    defining 63, 64
    source 65, 66
Bugzilla
    issues, handling 210, 212
    issues, identifying 210
    limitations 204
    limitations, fixing 205, 206
    URL 130, 203
Bugzilla Survey
    reference link 211
Bugzilla Usability Study
    reference link 211

C

codebase
    issues, solving 71-74
code complexity
    about 30
    clues 19
    handling, in software
        company 108-114

complexity

complexity
    about 87, 88, 90, 92
    accepting 89, 90
    changing 94, 95
    creating 21-24
    credibility 92, 93
    productivity, improving 96-98
compound complexity 67
computer 145, 147
consistency
    about 239
    maintaining 240
contributors
    obtaining 140, 142
    retaining, ways 130-136
counter-examples 164
Cycle of Observation
    accuracy 182
    completeness 182
    speed 182

D

design
    beginning 35, 36
determinism 196
developer hubris
    overcoming 235, 236

E

Eiffel
    URL 142
end to end testing 189, 190
engineer
    issues, solving 8

excellent software
  about 251
  behaving, as user expects 253
  complexity, adding 257
  user friendly 255
  user intention, communicating 256
  users intention,
      carrying out 252, 253
execution
  carrying out, in real world 249, 250

F

fakes 194, 195
fast programming
  keys 227, 228
future predictions
  accuracy 38, 40

I

information
  providing, to developers 242
instant gratification
  avoiding 245, 247
integration testing 190
ISAR
  in single line of code 156

K

keys, to fast programming
  caveat, for writing code 233
  distractions 232
  drawing 229, 230
  false ideas 233
  physical problems 231
  self-doubt 232
  starting 230
  step, skipping 231
  understanding 228

M

Mozilla
  URL 246

O

ODA cycle 183

P

power of no
  about 213-216
  bad ideas, recognizing 215
  clarifications 217, 218
privacy
  about 167, 174
  privacy of information 170-174
  privacy of space 168, 169
productivity 88
programmer
  about 5
  reasons, for creating
      complexity 219-224
programming
  developer productivity,
      measuring 106
  developer productivity, working 104
  lines of code 101, 102
  measured 100
  product is code 104
  productivity, defining 100
  software engineers 105
  valid metric, determining 102, 103

R

rabbit hole 75
real systems
  testing 193

refactoring
about 116, 118
determining 120, 121
results 156
right way 57-59
rockstar programmer
about 11
secret 12, 13

S

security
about 175
ways in, limiting 176
software
about 150, 151
as knowledge 160-162
software design
about 15
laws 60
software systems
about 124
code, reviewing 126
example 125
implementing 126
strictness 41-45
structure 153, 154

T

TDD cycle
about 180
development processes 181
productivity 181
technology
advance of technology,
importance 165

testing
about 185
assumptions 188
boundaries 187
conclusion 198
coverage 198
determinism 196
end to end testing 189, 190
fakes 194, 196
integration testing 190
reality 193
speed 197
unit testing 192
testing software 185
trust
providing, to developers 242
Two is Too Many rule
refactoring, scenario 49, 50

U

unit testing 192
users
issues, arising from 243, 244

V

VCI
URL 246

W

wrong way
about 52-54
analysis 55
group, bringing 56

Made in the USA
Lexington, KY
09 November 2017